SIGNS MAKE SENSE

HUMAN HORIZONS SERIES

SIGNS MAKE SENSE

A Guide to British Sign Language

CATH SMITH

Illustrated by David Hodgson

A CONDOR BOOK
SOUVENIR PRESS (E&A) LTD

First published 1990 by Souvenir Press (Educational & Academic) Ltd.
43 Great Russell Street, London WC1B 3PA

Reprinted 1991, 1992 (twice), 1993, 1994, 1995, 1996 (twice), 1997, 1998, 1999, 2000

ISBN 0 285 65083 1

Photoset and printed in Great Britain by
Redwood Books, Trowbridge, Wiltshire

ACKNOWLEDGEMENTS

First and foremost, my thanks to Dr Terry Morris, who initiated the work on *Communication Link: a dictionary of signs*, and for his kind permission to reproduce a selection of its contents. This dictionary provided an abundant reference of sign vocabulary and detail upon which to ponder, and through it I was able to structure *Signs Make Sense*.

A special thank you to my deaf and hearing colleagues who offered valued opinions and criticisms of this book in its early stages. Their backgrounds cover social work, teaching, parenthood, interpreting, research and deaf club chairing, and all, like myself, have at some point been students of BSL:

Mary Brennan
Judith Collins
Martin Colville
Peter Evans
Lorraine Fletcher
Rosemary Ottaway
Keith Williams

My gratitude to Mary Plackett, Chief Librarian of the Royal National Institute for the Deaf, for her assistance with details of publications and addresses of national organisations, and to Sarah Johnson, who helped me to complete the typing of the manuscript.

To countless individuals of the British Deaf Community I owe the biggest thanks of all — for the privilege of sharing your thoughts, attitudes and experiences. Your creative abilities, not to mention your tolerance of hearing learners, never cease to amaze me.

A personal thank you to my family for their support and encouragement.

Last, but by no means least, I would like to express my sincere indebtedness to Dave Hodgson, without whose skilful illustrations this book would not have been possible.

CONTENTS

APPENDICES

INTRODUCTION

British Sign Language (BSL) is the primary language of The Deaf Community of Britain, through which it has evolved as an *essential* and *valued* communication system. This rich and complex language is visual, gestural and spatial. By its very nature, it is able to convey information in a way that is particularly appropriate to this medium, and quite different from spoken language.

For hearing people whose first language is English, it is not always easy to comprehend a visual language. When learning foreign languages, we accept the validity of change in word order, ways of expressing tense, or idioms relative to that language, even though they are quite different from our native language. Yet many hearing people have difficulty accepting such differences in BSL, and want to use signs in a way that closely reflects English, feeling dissatisfied with what they consider to be inadequacies within the language.

In the past, such attitudes have led to a tendency to teach signs on a 'sign for a word' basis, and also to a tendency for deaf people to adapt their communication with hearing people, so that it more closely resembles English. Deaf people vary considerably in their use and understanding of English. Most feel more comfortable with, and understand more clearly, Sign Language as it is used within the deaf community.

The tendency to view BSL as an inferior system of communication, relying on random gesture and mime to convey telegram-like messages, has persisted, mainly due to lack of understanding of the very different rules and ways of conveying information visually.

In recent years, BSL has been the focus of research to analyse its underlying rules and structure. This has enabled those both teaching and learning the language to appreciate many factors which had hitherto been either overlooked, or dismissed as being unimportant or ungrammatical. The research, and publications which have ensued, are still in the process of unfolding and explaining the fascinating complexities of the language. This is gradually bringing about a change in attitude to BSL, and to the deaf community to which it belongs.

The intention of this book is to focus on some of the well-established principles of the language and, from this convenient reference point, to draw in some of the more recently identified features. It is hoped in this way to give an introductory feel for the language, and some understanding of the way *signs make sense*.

When we see BSL in fluent use, we can appreciate that the whole person is involved. Facial and bodily expression and movement, eye contact and gaze, lip pattern and the fluid movements of the signs themselves, all combine to form an integrated language system.

Using the written medium to introduce a language such as BSL has obvious restrictions. For example, some of the non-manual and spatial elements of the language are extremely difficult to illustrate and are best shown through demonstration in a signing class, or through face-to-face contact with deaf people. These elements, therefore, although vitally important to BSL, are outside the scope of this book.

However, the vocabulary of signs, the 'words' of the language, do provide a convenient focal point in this medium, in that they are more easily illustrated and explained.

For convenience, all the illustrations in this book have been given headings to enable identification and discussion. This can be somewhat misleading, and it is important to stress that many signs have more than one English translation. In addition, a variety of signs may be used for the same word depending on its meaning in different contexts.

It is also important to stress that the majority of signs illustrated are shown in their base form, and in isolation, similarly to words presented in an English dictionary. As with spoken English, signs in fluent everyday use are not performed exactly as shown within a dictionary and are liable to undergo certain changes.

Throughout the book, signs are presented in groups that have some connective meaning. For example, this may be the basic hand shape involved, or where the sign is located. It is hoped that such links between a sign's form and its meaning will provide a useful aid to understanding.

LINKS TO MEANING — SIGN RATIONALE

It is by no means always possible to give an explanation of a sign's origin, which will provide a direct link to its meaning. Despite this, a great many hearing people learning BSL do prefer to be given a 'rationale', or explanation, to help fix the sign in their memory.

Many explanations for the origins of signs are traditional and have been passed down by word of mouth. Such explanations cannot be regarded as reliable or scientifically proven, yet may still provide a useful aid to memory.

A good example of this is the sign **America**. Some years ago, I saw a BSL interpreter (Martin Colville) use this sign, which was completely new to me. Martin gave the rationale that the meshed fingers represent the United States, a perfectly reasonable and acceptable explanation which I passed on to others new to the sign.

AMERICA

Two open hands fingers meshed make horizontal circle in front of body.

Several years later, in June 1987, I read in the *British Deaf News* an interview with Mary Plackett, Chief Librarian of the Royal National Institute for the Deaf. Mary stated that the way she remembered signs was by their origins, and she gave **America** as an example, saying that she needed to think 'log cabin' to remember the position of the hands — the rationale that had been given to her as a learner.

Some time later, in *American Sign Language Dictionary* by Martin Sternberg, I was surprised to find this same sign with the rationale 'the fences built by the early settlers as protection against the Indians'.

These examples serve to illustrate that the way such links are explained, or put into words, may differ, yet they can still fulfil the useful purpose of providing a visual image which links a sign's formation to its meaning.

GUIDE TO CAPTIONS

In this book, signs and finger-spelling are described and drawn as if the person making them were right handed. Naturally, left handed people will sign and finger-spell using the left hand as the dominant hand.

The captions are intended to add extra information to explain the movement of the hands which cannot always be shown in a drawing. Where possible, a full description of the sign is given, but in some cases the hand shapes may not be given if they are clear from the drawing.

To avoid misunderstandings, and lengthy descriptions, we have used set terms to describe:

1 Parts of the hand.
2 Common hand shapes.
3 Directions.

PARTS OF THE HAND

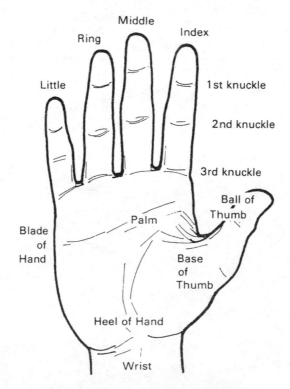

The right hand is always written as R.
The left hand is always written as L.

BASIC HAND SHAPES

Flat Hand

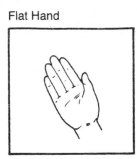

Open Hand

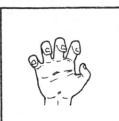

Clawed Hand

Fist

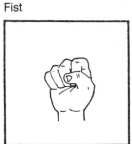

Closed Hand

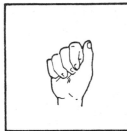

Bent Hand

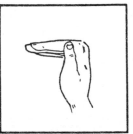

Bunched Hand

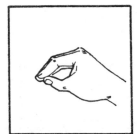

'O' hand

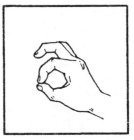

Cupped Hand

Full 'O' Hand

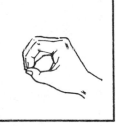

Hand shapes based on the **Right** hand shape of British two-handed finger spelling.

'C' Hand

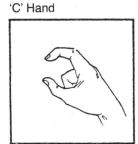

Full 'C' Hand

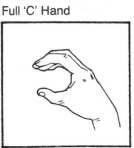

'M' Hand

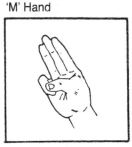

'N' Hand

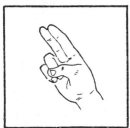

'R' Hand

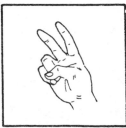

'V' Hand

These are the most common hand shapes, but do not cover every shape used in signing. They may be further clarified, e.g. R. hand loosely cupped, L. hand slightly bent, two 'V' hands, fingers bent, etc.

If the caption says, e.g. index, middle finger and thumb extended, then it is understood that the other fingers are closed.

DIRECTIONS

The terms used to describe the directions in which the hands are facing, pointing and moving, are as follows:

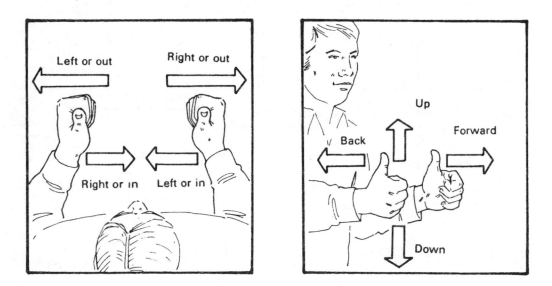

FACING
The direction in which the palm of the hand faces is given as 'palm up', 'palm back', etc., even if the hand is closed.

In the above illustrations, the R. hand is palm left, the L. hand is palm right. They may also be described as palms facing.

POINTING
The hand may be described as 'pointing' up, forward, etc., even if the fingers are bent in a different direction, or closed.

In the above illustrations, both hands are pointing forward, thumbs up.

MOVEMENT
Where a movement or position is diagonal, it is described as 'forward/left', 'back/right', etc.

Many movements are described as 'hands move **alternately**'. This means that they move at the same time in opposite directions, as in 'up and down', or continuously in the same circular direction, alternately.

Some signs need a full description of hand shapes and positions before any movement is made. This is then called a **formation**. This means they keep their position together as they move.

GUIDE TO DRAWINGS

The following types of arrows mean:

A broken movement.

Movement in one direction then the other.

Repeated movement.

Hands move apart.

The sign ends with stress.

Hand or fingers open then close.

Open hand closes.

Closed hand opens.

Impact on point drawn.

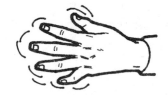

Very small repeated movements.

Hands drawn in dotted lines show the **start** of the sign. Hands drawn in solid lines show the **finish**.

Signs that are mimed actions of holding objects may have the object drawn in dotted lines to help people understand and remember them.

Section One

ICONICITY

explained, does give a definite link to meaning.

Some examples of these are dealt with in separate sections and are presented in groups based on **hand shapes** and sign **locations** that have conventionalised links to meaning. The section on **time** looks at the way space, direction and movement can be used to express passages of time, in a visual way.

ICONICITY: SHAPE

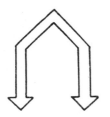

Some signs are very obviously **iconic**, that is, they clearly look like the object they represent.

These are some examples of signs that represent objects by giving a visual description of their **shape**.

Curved fingers are commonly used to indicate curved objects, and occur here in **ball** and **bottle**, to indicate the curved surfaces of these objects.

Flat hands are commonly used to indicate flat objects, and occur here in **book**, **box** and **table**, to indicate the flat surfaces of these objects.

As previously mentioned, not all of these objects look exactly like the stereotyped representation given in the sign, but the sign has become conventionalised, and can be used to depict any house, table, and so on.

It is possible to modify some of these signs to give more specific information when a particular object is being referred to — for example, a 'big ball', or a 'long table', in which the sign is made bigger, or longer, respectively.

BALL

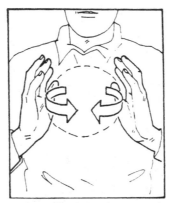

Fingers of both hands open and curved; hands swivel to touch thumbs then little fingers, to indicate shape of ball.

BOTTLE

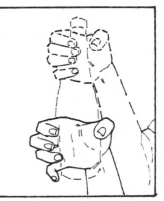

R. hand, fingers curved, moves downwards as thumb opens to indicate shape of bottle.

BOOK

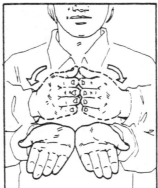

Two flat hands pointing forward, palm to palm, open to palms up.

BOX

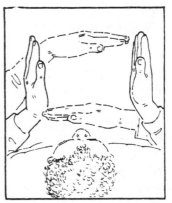

Flat hands palms back, L. in front of R., move to palms facing indicating sides of box.

TABLE

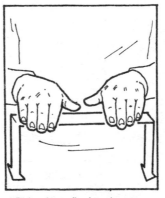

Palm down flat hands move apart, twist to palms facing and move down to indicate shape of table.

HOUSE

Indicate shape of house, with two 'N' hands.

ICONICITY: OUTLINE

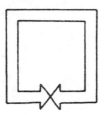

Other signs give a visual image of the object they represent by defining the **outline**. These are very similar to the first group, in that the shape is described, but these examples show the index finger/s or thumb and index being used.

Some of these signs can again change in context, for example, **picture** can be made large or small, square, oblong, or circular, when a particular picture is being referred to.

The size and shape of the movement should be relevant to that object, so that the difference between **cheque** and **ticket**, for example, is shown in the relative size, even though the hand shape and movement are the same. Context is also important in clarifying meaning.

Further details of the importance of context, and examples of how signs can change accordingly, can be found in Section Two.

PICTURE

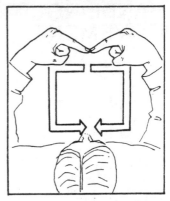

Indexes make outline of picture.

ROOM

Indexes pointing down move out, back, then in, to indicate outline of room.

PLATE

R. index makes a circle over L. palm.

RULER

Indexes and thumbs pull apart indicating shape of a ruler.

CHEQUE

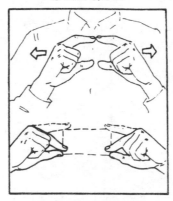

Indicate outline of cheque with indexes and thumbs of both hands.

TICKET

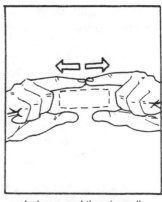

Indexes and thumbs pull slightly apart, to indicate shape of ticket.

ICONICITY: HANDLING/ MOVEMENT

This group of signs represents the **handling** and/or **movement** associated with a particular object.

The hand shape in these and many more handling signs is particularly important, not merely in terms of the shape and size, but in the angle, position and movement, which should accurately reflect that particular object in use.

Most people new to signing would have no difficulty in identifying the meaning of the whole group of iconic signs so far mentioned, and many would be able to produce signs for these objects before being shown the accepted sign. Encouraging people to use the abilities they already possess is a good way of establishing confidence.

Grasping the basic idea of iconicity stimulates imagination and inventiveness and should encourage the use of signs in context in ways that make good sense visually.

APPLE

Mime holding apple in front of mouth, twist from wrist as if taking a bite.

BANANA

Mime holding and peeling a banana.

BAT

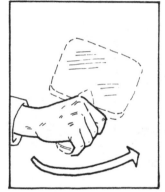

Mime holding and striking with a bat.

CAR

Mime holding and moving a steering wheel.

IRON

Mime holding an iron and ironing.

SAUCE

Mime shaking sauce from a bottle.

ICONICITY: PLACEMENT

RELATIVE POSITIONING

Visual imagery, as evident here in the prepositions **in**, **on**, **under** and **over**, can show the *position* of objects or people in relation to other things.

Prepositions are not always used to show positioning, however. A crucial feature of BSL is the 'placement' of signs in space, corresponding to their position in reality.

The information conveyed here, in the signs **fire** and **picture**, shows that the picture is located above, or over the fire. This is shown in the way one sign is placed above the other, equivalent to 'a picture over the fire' in English. The signed version does not need the addition of the sign **over**, as this information is given in the way the signs are positioned.

The last example shows the position of a book on a shelf, by placing the sign **book** above the sign **shelf**. Their relative positions are given visually, without the need for the sign **on**, which would be essential to give the equivalent information in English.

These examples give some indication of the language differences between BSL and English.

IN

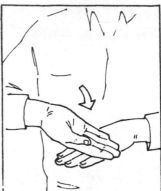

R. flat hand makes short movement forward/under L.

ON

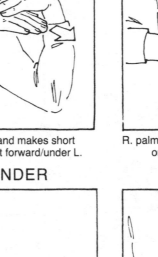

R. palm up flat hand placed down onto back of L. hand.

UNDER

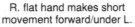

R. flat hand moves under L. in small arc.

OVER

R. hand slightly bent arcs over L. hand.

PICTURE OVER FIRE

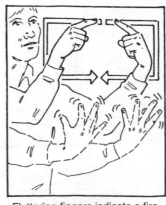

Fluttering fingers indicate a fire, then indexes trace outline of a picture above it.

BOOK ON SHELF

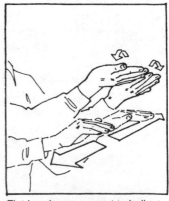

Flat hands move apart to indicate a shelf, then palms together hands open to indicate a book directly above.

ICONICITY: MOVEMENT

The examples of iconic signs looked at so far have shown the visual representation of concrete ideas, or objects. In most of these, the link between a sign's formation and its meaning is quite readily apparent.

However, it does seem to be the case that abstract concepts can also involve a degree of iconicity to represent meaning in ways that appear to be visually appropriate.

For example, the repeated waggling, or wavering, movements shown here in **perhaps** and **any**, seem very appropriate to the indefinite connotations of these words.

In **must** and **should**, the movement is both sharp and emphatic, which appears to stress the idea of insistence and obligation.

A definite, emphatic movement occurs again, in **sure**, to convey the idea of certainty, whilst the wavering movement in **not sure** seems aptly to convey the idea of uncertainty and doubt.

PERHAPS

R. thumb and little finger extended, palm left. Hand waggles with quick twisting movement of wrist.

ANY

R. closed hand, thumb and little finger extended, sweeps from left to right in front of body whilst waggling.

MUST

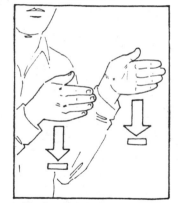

Flat hands held parallel move sharply down with stress.

SHOULD

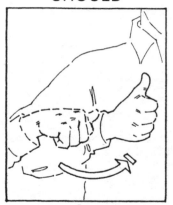

R. closed hand, palm down, thumb extended and pointing left, moves sharply in, twisting to palm back, thumb up, with emphasis.

SURE

Blade of R. flat hand strikes L. palm, sharply.

NOT SURE

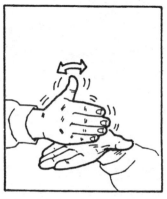

R. hand makes small side to side wavering movements whilst resting on L. palm.

ICONICITY: NEGATIVE SIGNS

The movement in the *negative* signs illustrated here also seems to be a significant indicator of meaning, tending to move *away* from the head or body.

Facial and bodily expressions are obviously important in conveying the negative aspects of these signs and to show degree and intensity.

There is a variety of ways of expressing negative ideas. These are just some examples, which show the negative forms of a number of signs that appear in their positive forms in later sections.

See: 'believe' p. 65, 'agree' p. 48, 'know' p. 46, 'like' p. 79, 'want' p. 79, and 'will' p. 42.

DON'T BELIEVE

As for 'believe' (see p. 65), finishing with R. hand brushing sharply off L. hand.

DISAGREE

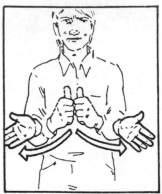

Hands start together, thumbs extended, then swing apart as fingers open in sharp movement.

DON'T KNOW

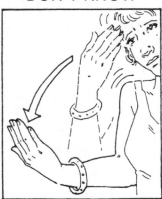

Tips of flat hand touch forehead, then move forward/down, with slight shrug of shoulders and shake of head.

DON'T LIKE

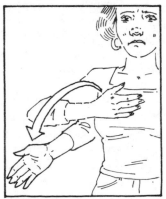

Flat hand on chest brushes up slightly and twists over, moving sharply away from body.

DON'T WANT

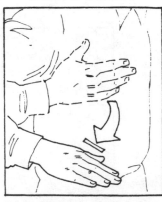

Flat hand, on side of upper chest, brushes sharply down and away from body, with emphasis.

WON'T

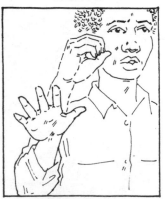

Fingers flexed behind thumb, hand moves sharply forward/down, from side of chin, and springs open.

ICONICITY: POINTING

Pointing is the basis for a number of BSL signs. These include pronouns, enabling a way of indicating people and objects without naming them.

Me, **you**, **she**, **her**, **he**, **him** and so on, are all indicated by pointing, as are **this**, **that**, **here** and **there**.

When more than one person or object is being indicated, as in **these**, **those**, **they**, **them** and **you** plural, the index finger swings from side to side whilst pointing towards the objects or people being referred to, as in **those**, illustrated here.

Parts of the body, such as **eye**, **ear**, **nose** and **mouth**, are also indicated by pointing.

HERE

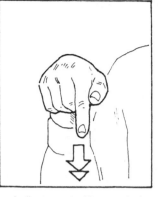

Indicate spot with extended index finger pointing down twice.

I

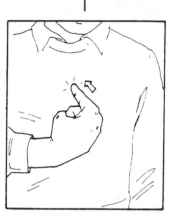

Point to self.

THAT

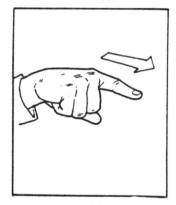

Index points forward, or to object or person concerned.

THIS

Indicate object with one downward movement of index.

THOSE

Index swings from side to side, pointing to objects or persons concerned.

YOU

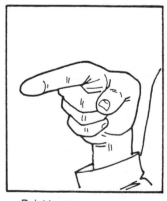

Point to person or persons concerned.

Section Two

SIGN VARIATIONS

INTRODUCTION

Information is conveyed visually within BSL by a combination of media, such as facial and bodily expression, movement, the use of space, and signs. The 'words' of the language, that is, the signs themselves, are just one part of a complex system of imparting information visually. The vital information-carrying elements vary little between individuals, but although *most* signs are standard throughout the country, there are variations, just as there are within spoken language.

BSL has evolved through the deaf community as an essential and valued communication system. This has given rise to variations due to factors such as geographical area or school background, or may reflect individual choice and style.

Many learners are put off or confused by the variety of signs for some words, and prefer to be given just one form of a sign, but this is to miss the whole point. Communication is *two*-way. It is not enough to learn how to perform signs, it is equally important to understand deaf people, and to appreciate the value and richness of their language, of which such variations are a part.

The previous section has hopefully given some insight into the way signs can create a visual representation of an object or an idea, based on shape, or an associated action, such as handling. This section looks at how variations can arise in the *form* of signs whilst still remaining within the conventionally accepted representations, and includes some examples of regional variations.

Signs may also vary because the *meaning* of words can change in context. *Different signs* may be used for the same word, depending on its meaning, or a sign may be modified to give specific detail appropriate to the context in which it is used. Details of such changes are given in the following pages, including examples of the way facial expression can change meaning.

Some signs, notably **numbers** and **colours**, are subject to wide regional variation, and are not included. Local signing classes and contact with the deaf community will provide the necessary clarification of what is accepted as standard within a particular area.

SIGN VARIATIONS: ICONICITY

By considering the strong element of visual imagery within BSL, as illustrated by the iconic signs so far considered, it is possible to see how variations might arise. The examples looked at have shown representation based on outline, shape, and associated actions.

The variations of the sign **banana**, illustrated here, show one version based on holding and peeling a banana, and the other based on its shape.

Dog is depicted in the first example by representing the legs in a 'begging' position, and in the second by patting the thigh, as if calling a dog.

The whiskers of a cat are chosen as the representative feature in the first illustration of **cat**, whilst the action of stroking a cat is indicated in the second.

These examples show that it is possible to represent ideas in more than one way and yet still remain within the accepted forms described in Section One dealing with visual imagery. The link between *form* and *meaning* in these signs remains quite clear, and allows choice of expression, just as in spoken language.

Not all signs have such clear links to meaning, but understanding the basis of signs can be of great benefit in appreciating how variations can arise.

BANANA

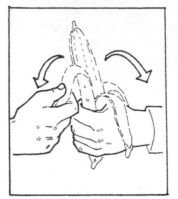

Mime holding and peeling a banana.

BANANA

Open indexes and thumbs move apart and close in the shape of a banana.

DOG

Two 'N' hands pointing down, move up and down slightly, like dog begging.

DOG

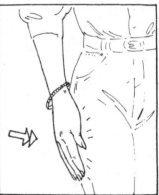

Pat thigh with flat hand, as if calling a dog.

CAT

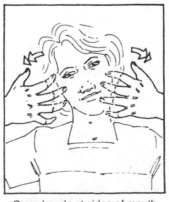

Open hands at sides of mouth move out slightly twice whilst flexing to indicate whiskers.

CAT

R. cupped hand strokes down the back of L. closed hand several times.

SIGN VARIATIONS: CHOICE

Within spoken language, we have an abundant choice of expressions at our disposal, to add interest and variety to our ideas. To describe a simple action like 'walk', for example, we might choose words such as hike, pace, go on foot, step out, take Shanks's pony, and so on.

We can also choose words that describe walking in more specific detail: plod, stroll, creep, wander, swagger, saunter, and so on.

BSL also offers an abundant choice of expression, both in the *form* of the sign, as shown in the illustrations here, and in the *way* it is made, to give specific detail in a visual way.

The different *forms* of the sign can be compared to using different words, such as 'go on foot' to mean 'walk'. The *way* it is signed can be compared to using words such as 'plod', to give more precise detail, as described on p. 36.

All the signs illustrated can be used to indicate 'walk' in general terms, and may be chosen as a matter of personal choice, or to add interest and variety.

The first illustration shows the index and middle fingers representing the legs in the action of walking. This sign is often offered to beginners because of its direct simplicity and, certainly, deaf people shown this sign would understand its meaning, although not all of them would sign it this way themselves. The other examples show some of the variations that may be used.

WALK

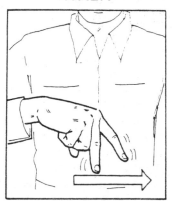

Index and middle fingers move like legs walking.

WALK

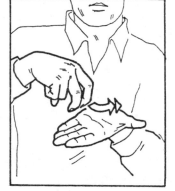

Tips of R. bent 'V' hand brush forward repeatedly along upturned L. palm.

WALK

Palm down R. 'N' hand makes small repeated brushing movement along fingers of palm down L. 'N' hand.

WALK

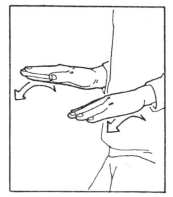

Palm down flat hands move alternately in small forward arcs to represent the feet in walking.

WALK

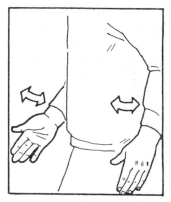

Flat hands swing forward and back alternately near sides of body.

SIGN VARIATIONS: DETAIL

As previously mentioned, all the various forms of **walk** can be used to indicate walking in general terms. However, it does seem to be the case that some forms of **walk** are more appropriate to some contexts than others, or that the *way* they are signed can be easily modified to suit some contexts rather than others.

The following examples are intended to show the basic idea of the type of context to which they may be appropriate, and how they might be modified.

The first illustration might be used in contexts such as 'the baby is now walking' or 'I walked round and round', in which the hand moves round in a horizontal circle as the fingers move in the action of legs 'walking'.

The swinging movement of the arms in the second illustration can be modified quite aptly to describe, for example, 'strolling', or taking a 'brisk walk', depending on the type of movement and appropriate facial and bodily expression.

The last illustration gives a closer, more detailed perspective of the feet in the action of walking, and lends itself very appropriately to contexts that require such detail, as in 'creeping quietly', or 'treading carefully', for example. Again, it is not only the way the sign is made, but facial and bodily expression that convey this extra information.

More than one form of the sign may be used in the same conversation, or 'text', to allow more specific detail to be conveyed. An example of this would be 'the baby is now walking (first illustration) — she just stood up and walked yesterday (last illustration)'. This change allows detailed information, in the way the hands move, to show a baby's first tentative steps.

References to sign variations and examples of context are given, wherever possible, throughout the book, either with illustrations, or in the comments.

WALK

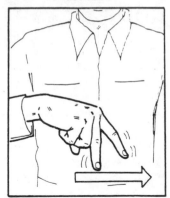

Index and middle fingers move like legs walking.

WALK

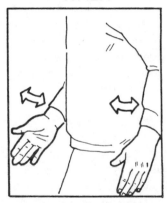

Flat hands swing forward and back alternately near sides of body.

WALK

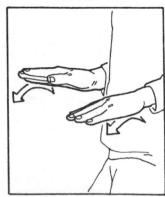

Palm down flat hands move alternately in small forward arcs to represent the feet in walking.

SIGN VARIATIONS: CONTEXT

THE IMPORTANCE OF CONTEXT

Many English words have different meanings which rely on context to distinguish their meaning.

In signing, it is the *meaning* that is important, not the words, and so it is essential to consider the true meaning to be conveyed, to ensure that the visual information is appropriate to the context.

This can be a difference in a word's basic meanings, as in the first two examples here of the word **light**.

The first sign is used to mean the opposite of 'dark' and would be used in contexts such as 'it's still light', 'light blue', and so on.

The second is used to indicate the opposite of 'heavy', as in 'this box is light', and so on.

All the other examples are variations of **light** meaning a source of illumination. Because of the iconic nature of the sign, in which the opening fingers represent rays of light, it makes good visual sense for this sign to change, in location, direction and size of movement, to give a more accurate visual description of different lights, like the ones illustrated.

There are many others — for example, the lights on a Christmas tree, a flashing light door bell, the light on a police car, and so on, which would also be signed in a visually appropriate way.

The importance of context cannot be overstated and will be referred to throughout the book, with examples wherever possible.

LIGHT (dark)

Palm back flat hands, start crossed, then swing apart to point up.

LIGHT (weight)

Palm up flat hands make repeated light upward movement.

LIGHT (lamp)

Full 'O' hand moves in slightly as it springs open at head height.

TRAFFIC LIGHTS

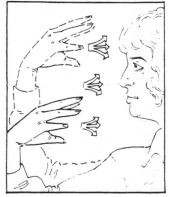

Hand held away from body, palm back, fingers spring open from full 'O' hand; repeat twice, moving hand down slightly each time. Both hands may be used.

HEADLIGHTS

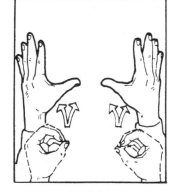

Fingers of both hands spring open from full 'O' hands with slight forward movement to indicate car headlights.

INDICATOR

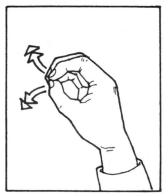

Fingers make small repeated opening movements from full 'O' hand, to the right or left.

SIGN VARIATIONS: REGIONAL DIFFERENCES

The variations in signs looked at so far in this section have shown a selection of iconic signs in which different features have been chosen to represent objects, actions or ideas.

Not all signs have this strong element of visual imagery by which variations can be easily explained. However, it does help to remember that facial expression, lip-pattern and context can help enormously when new and unfamiliar signs are encountered.

Alternative forms of signs provide choice and variety of expression. Some versions of signs are particularly common within different parts of the country, in a way that is comparable to accent and dialect in spoken language.

The illustrations on this page show common regional variations in the signs **boy** and **who**. Although slightly different, all the signs for **boy** are made on the chin, possibly to indicate a smooth chin, (the sign 'man' involves stroking the chin to indicate a beard).

Two variations of **who** shown on this page are also made on the chin, possibly to draw attention to the distinctive lip-pattern of the word. The circling index finger in the last example is also used to mean 'someone', and facial expression is important to clarify its use in question form, together with eye gaze or pointing.

BOY

Brush R. index pointing left across chin.

BOY

Tips of 'N' hand brush down chin, twice.

BOY

Index closes onto thumb, in a stroking movement, down the chin.

WHO

Index edge of 'R' hand contacts chin.

WHO

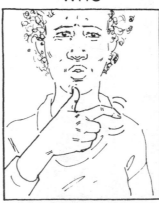

Index and thumb extended, thumb tip contacts chin as the index flexes, several times.

WHO

Extended index finger moves in small horizontal circles.

SIGN VARIATIONS: QUESTIONS

This version of **who** is also made on the chin, but although **who** has a number of variations, the other 'question' words illustrated here do appear to be standard throughout the country.

Where can involve one hand, or two, and **which** changes direction in context, as illustrated on p. 40, but these are not regional differences.

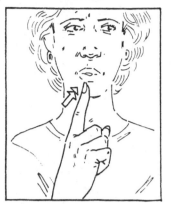

R. index extended, palm left, taps chin, twice.

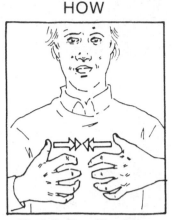

HOW

Knock 2nd knuckles of two clawed hands together twice.

WHAT

Index pointing up, palm forward, shakes from side to side, in small, quick movement.

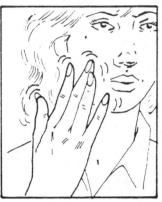

WHEN

Fingers flutter at side of chin.

WHY

Edge of R. index taps left shoulder, twice.

WHERE

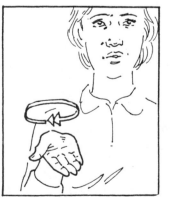

Palm up flat hand moves in small vertical circles.

WHICH

Thumb and little finger extended, hand moves from side to side, or between the items referred to.

SIGN VARIATIONS: DIRECTION CHANGES IN CONTEXT

WHICH

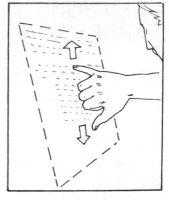

Little finger and thumb extended from closed hand, moves up and down between the items in question.

It was pointed out on the previous page that **which** changes direction in context, and this requires illustrated examples.

The changes signs may undergo in context, such as 'walk' (p. 35) and 'light' (p. 37), show that such changes are necessary to make good visual sense in different contexts. A sign such as **which** is not as obviously iconic as these examples, but the movement of the hand indicates a choice between two or more items. Again, it makes good visual sense for this movement to change direction, to indicate the items in question in any particular context.

For example, if the alternatives are items on a list, the hand would move up and down the list, to show that the choice is between those items. This is illustrated in the first example.

If the question related to items located in front of the signer, as in the second example, the movement would again indicate the choice between these items.

The third illustration shows the movement between the signer and another person, and indicates 'which one of us'.

The directional changes would apply even if the items were not there, but had been previously referred to.

WHICH

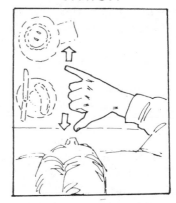

Little finger and thumb extended from closed hand, moves backwards and forwards between the items in question.

WHICH

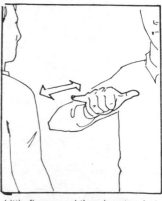

Little finger and thumb extended from closed hand, moves to and fro between the people in queston.

SIGN VARIATIONS: FACIAL EXPRESSION

Facial expression is a vital element in BSL and is constantly referred to throughout this book.

It is important, at this stage, to look in more detail at how facial expression can alter the meaning of some signs.

These illustrations show how a questioning expression can change the meaning of **age** to **how old**? In the same way, **many** becomes **how many**?, and **reason** changes to **why**?, when signed with a questioning expression.

There are many, many ways in which facial expression can convey, modify or change meaning, other than question forms. These examples are intended to give just the basic idea.

People vary greatly in their natural, physical expressiveness, and there is a tendency for people new to signing to concentrate on the hands, that is, the signs themselves.

As already pointed out, the signs are only one feature in a complex and integrated system of giving information visually. The other crucial elements, including facial and bodily expression, need constant reinforcement in signing classes.

AGE

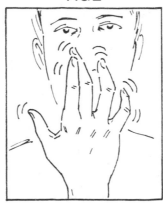

Fingers of open hand flutter in front of nose.

HOW OLD

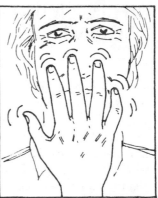

Fingers of open hand flutter in front of nose with questioning facial expression.

MANY

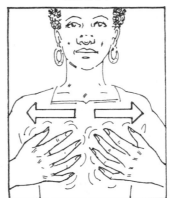

Open hands move apart, fingers fluttering.

HOW MANY

Fingers of open hands flutter as hands move apart, with questioning facial expression.

REASON

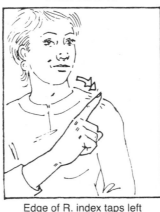

Edge of R. index taps left shoulder, twice.

WHY

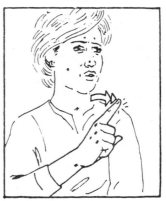

Edge of R. index taps left shoulder, with questioning facial expression.

SIGN VARIATIONS: INFORMAL VARIATIONS

The final examples in this section dealing with sign variations illustrate the use of signs within fluent communication, as may be found in social or informal situations.

In spoken language, the way we speak and use words varies from the precise and exact version that may be found in a dictionary, or book of grammar.

Most of the illustrations given in this, and other books concerning sign vocabulary, give a precise description of each sign in isolation.

In fluent usage, particularly in informal settings, signs become fluid, and less exact than the 'dictionary version', just as words are run together and contracted in speech.

The first illustration shows the sign **can**, located in front of the face. This can be regarded as the 'dictionary version' of the sign. The second illustration shows the same hand shape and movement, but this version is located lower down, a change often occurring in relaxed conversation.

A similar change can occur in **don't know**, from its usual location starting on the forehead, to a smaller, contracted movement, and **will** may be made lower down than its usual location at the side of the chin.

CAN

R. 'C' hand palm back in front of face – pull away from face and flex fingers slightly.

CAN

'C' hand held away from body, moves down slightly, as fingers flex.

DON'T KNOW

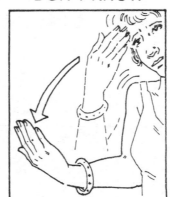

Tips of flat hand touch forehead, then move forward/down, with slight shrug of shoulders and shake of head.

DON'T KNOW

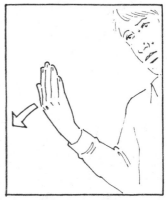

Palm back flat hand makes small movement forward/down with appropriate facial and bodily expression.

WILL

Palm forward closed hand twists forward at side of chin.

WILL

Palm forward closed hand twists forward.

Section Three

HAND SHAPES WITH LINKS
TO MEANING

INTRODUCTION

Researchers have identified approximately 60 hand shapes within British Sign Language. It is outside the scope of this book to consider all of these, but attention is given to about a dozen commonly occurring significant hand shapes in two main groups.

This section looks at those hand shapes that have a common link to meaning, while Section Five looks at hand shapes used to directly represent people and vehicles.

Some hand shapes are particularly significant in that the hand shape itself conveys meaning. The closed hand with the thumb extended provides the base sign **good**. This same hand shape frequently occurs in signs that have pleasant or *positive* connotations. This is not always the case, but is a general principle that may help learners to understand and remember this group of signs.

The little finger extended from a closed hand provides the base sign **bad**. The same hand shape often occurs in signs with unpleasant or *negative* connotations.

The **clawed hand** commonly appears in meanings expressing *tension* or agitation.

A **closed hand** directed towards the person concerned is used to indicate *possession*.

Finally, in this section, an open hand with the **fingers fluttering** occurs in signs relating to *number* in some form, particularly the questioning of number.

As with all signs, facial and bodily expression, the specific movement involved, the direction in which the hand faces and where it is located, all combine to give further information. In this section relevant details are given in the comments alongside the illustrations whenever possible, and Section Four looks in more detail at the significant way some signs are located on different parts of the head or body, and how these are linked to meaning.

GOOD

BAD

CLAWED

CLOSED

FLUTTERING FINGERS

'GOOD' HAND SHAPE

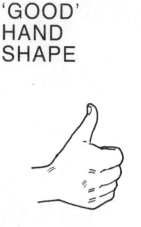

Signs that have *positive* or pleasant associations frequently incorporate the hand shape used in the sign **good**, in which the thumb is extended from a closed hand.

This is not always the case, but is a general principle that can help to give a connective meaning to this group of signs.

Many signs can be *modified*, that is altered slightly to differentiate or qualify the degree and intensity to be expressed. For example, the sign **good** can be modified by appropriate facial and bodily expression, to indicate 'quite good', 'great', 'excellent', and so on. Both hands can be used for extra emphasis.

Appropriate facial and bodily expression are crucial elements in expressing such differences in intensity.

The *location* of the hand shape, and the specific movement involved, combine to give further information. For example, the base sign **good** is located in neutral space, in front of the body. In this form, it is also a common greeting sign in the deaf community. **Know** and **clever** are located on the forehead, the most common location for signs connected with mental activity.

The movement in **clever** is sharp, appropriate to the idea of a sharp mind, or of mental skill. The movement in **skill** is also sharp, and its location off the left palm is appropriate to this sign's use to imply manual, or other forms of dexterity.

GOOD

Thumb held up.

KNOW

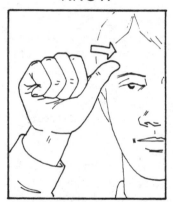

Tip of extended thumb touches side of forehead.

CLEVER

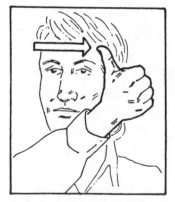

R. thumb moves across forehead in sharp movement.

SKILL

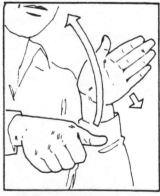

L. flat hand, palm right, makes slight downward movement, as R. thumb sweeps sharply up L. palm.

'GOOD' HAND SHAPE

The 'good' hand shape appears here following a circling movement round the face in **handsome** and **pretty**.

Lovely has similar connotations and is sometimes located under the eye, or off the cheek.

Nice involves this hand shape moving across the chin, near the mouth. The sign is also used to mean 'delicious', or to express something agreeable or pleasant in any sense.

Brave and **well** are both located on the body, where signs expressing feelings and emotions are most commonly located. In **brave**, the 'good' hand shape is formed in a forward movement following contact with the body by the flat hand.

Well relates to physical well-being and is very commonly used in greeting form, with a questioning facial expression to indicate, 'Are you well?' or, 'How are you?'

HANDSOME

Index circles round face then moves out to closed hand, thumb up.

PRETTY

Index circles face, then hand moves out slightly, thumb up.

LOVELY

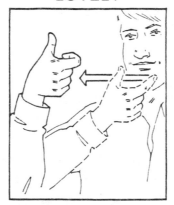

R. index and thumb extended; draw index slowly under bottom lip left to right and close index, leaving thumb up.

NICE

R. thumb moves across chin from left to right.

BRAVE

R. flat hand on chest, moves forward to closed hand, thumb extended in sharp movement.

WELL

Thumbs move down upper chest, then twist forward.

'GOOD' HAND SHAPE

The body is again the location for **courage** and **fit**. In **courage**, the 'good' hand shapes are formed in a forward movement following contact with the body by the fingertips. This sign is also used as a variation of 'confident'.

Holy, and this version of **all right**, involve a circling movement with this hand shape which then contacts the left palm. Another common variation of 'all right' involves both hands in this hand shape, with the thumbs up, moving in small circles.

In **agree** and **suit**, the hands come together in a way that seems appropriate to the idea of agreement and co-operation.

COURAGE

Contact trunk with fingertips, then move hands forward, closing sharply to closed hands, thumbs extended.

FIT (healthy)

Thumbs brush down upper trunk, then move away from body and twist out slightly.

HOLY

R. closed hand, thumb out, makes large anti-clockwise circle above L. palm, then drops down onto L. palm.

ALL RIGHT

R. closed hand, thumb extended, makes clockwise circle above L. palm, then comes down onto L. palm.

AGREE

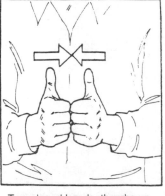

Two closed hands, thumbs up, held about 6″ apart, move together and touch.

SUIT

Closed hands, thumbs extended, move in to contact each other.

'GOOD' HAND SHAPE

The types of movement made by the hands in the 'good' hand shapes illustrated here in **better** and **best** do seem to be appropriate in conveying the comparative aspects of **better**, in which the thumbs contact twice, and the superlative quality expressed by the single emphatic movement in **best**.

The idea of a comparative choice or preference is echoed again in the repeated movement in **rather** and **favourite**.

In **regular**, the movement of this hand shape behind the left palm is an indication of an ongoing passage of time, described in more detail in Section Six.

The hands move down the body in **smart** to indicate smart clothing.

BETTER

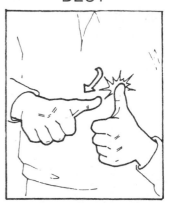

R. thumb strikes tip of L. thumb twice in a forward movement.

BEST

R. thumb strikes tip of L. thumb once in forward movement.

RATHER

R. closed hand, thumb extended, contacts L. palm twice.

FAVOURITE

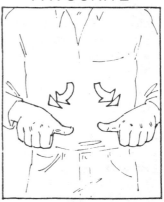

Two closed hands, thumbs extended, make two jerky movements forward/down.

REGULAR

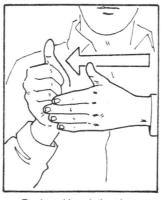

R. closed hand, thumb up, brushes along palm back L. hand.

SMART

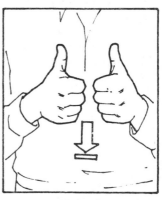

Hands held on chest, thumbs up, make short movement down, with stress.

'GOOD' HAND SHAPE

Both hands using the 'good' hand shape appear in this group of signs.

In **proud**, the hands move backwards alternately to contact the signer's body to indicate the subjective feeling of pride.

All the others involve a forward movement, as in the small repeated circling movements in **popular**, and the larger, more deliberate movements in **congratulate** and **praise**, to express praise being conveyed forward, to another person.

Both hands move forward simultaneously in **support** and **encourage**, in a way that seems to imply pushing or encouraging. An alternative sign for 'encourage' involves two open hands, pointing forward/down, palms forward making the same repeated forward movement.

PROUD

Thumbs brush down chest in alternate backward circles.

POPULAR

Both thumbs extended, hands move quickly in small alternate forward circles.

CONGRATULATE

Two closed hands, thumbs extended, make forward circles alternately.

PRAISE

Both thumbs up, hands make alternate forward circles at head height.

SUPPORT

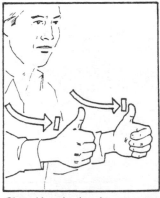

Closed hands, thumbs up, move forward in small arc, with stress.

ENCOURAGE

Both hands, thumbs up, push forwards twice simultaneously.

'GOOD' HAND SHAPE

The 'good' hand shape in **right** is palm down as it contacts the left palm. In its base form, as in the top illustration, it can be used to indicate 'correct', 'proper' or as in the sense of a legal claim, 'it's her *right*'.

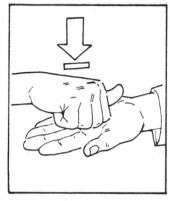

R. closed hand, thumb extended, bangs L. palm with emphasis.

YOU'RE RIGHT

R. closed hand with thumb extended, directed palm towards the person concerned.

I'M RIGHT

This sign changes direction in context, as in **you're right** and **I'm right**, illustrated here. 'She/he's right' would involve this same hand shape directed palm towards the person concerned.

Closed hand with thumb extended, taps chest twice.

BLESS

The idea of conferring a right, or sanctifying, is implied in the downward movement of both hands in **bless**. This sign is also used more generally to indicate sanction, confirmation and approval, as shown here in **approve**.

As pointed out in the Introduction, all the signs in this book have been given headings to enable identification, and are not to be regarded as the sign's sole meaning.

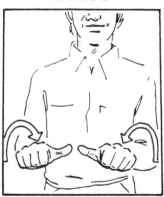

Two closed hands, thumbs extended, palms up. Move up slightly and twist over to finish palms down.

APPROVE

Palm down closed hands, thumbs extended, make downward movement.

'GOOD' HAND SHAPE

Like a good many signs, the last one illustrated in this whole group of signs involving the 'good' hand shape does not have a single English equivalent. The meaning of this sign is entirely determined by the context in which it appears.

Succeed expresses some of its meanings, in the sense of getting one's wish, or accomplishing what is attempted. It can also imply something done or completed, or can convey the sense of managing to overcome a difficulty, or of something finally coming to fruition, or turning out well.

SUCCEED

Two closed hands, thumbs extended, twist from palms facing to palms down and pull slightly apart, in quick movement.

'BAD' HAND SHAPE

Signs that have *negative* or unpleasant connotations frequently incorporate the hand shape used in the sign **bad**.

Again, this is not always the case, but is a general principle that can help to give a connective meaning to this group of signs.

The sign **bad** can be modified to show intensity. Appropriate facial and bodily expression can indicate 'awful', 'terrible' and so on. Both hands can be used for extra emphasis.

The location of the hand shape, and the specific movement involved, combine to give further information.

For example, **suspicious**, with its implication of mistrust, is located on the forehead, commonly the location for signs expressing mental activity in some form.

The location of this hand shape is near the mouth in **sour** and **bitter**, to give an indication of a disagreeable taste, whereas the forward movement from the mouth in **swear** implies bad language.

BAD

Little finger held up.

SUSPICIOUS

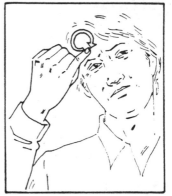

Little finger makes small circular movements on forehead.

SOUR

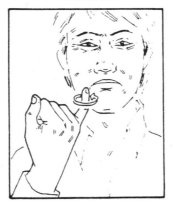

Little finger of R. hand, palm left, twists to palm back at corner of mouth.

BITTER

Make small circle on chin with tip of little finger.

SWEAR

Little finger moves forward from mouth with emphasis.

UGLY

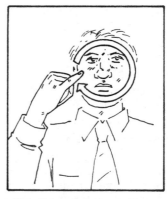

Little finger circles round face.

'BAD' HAND SHAPE

The types of movement made by the hands in the 'bad' hand shape shown here can be compared to the examples of 'best' and 'better' given on p. 49. In this case the single emphatic movement is used to express **worst** and the repeated contact to convey the comparative aspects of **worse**.

An alternative form of 'worse' starts with the little fingers contacting, then pulling apart in a downward movement in a way which also seems to be appropriate to the idea of deterioration.

A downward movement occurs again in **spoil**, **fail**, **ill** and **weak**, which seems to add to the negative connotations of these signs.

In **fail**, the fingers twist down and apart, giving the idea of something falling away, or of loss.

The hands move down the body in this version of **ill**, to convey physical illness. This sign is also used to express tiredness or general malaise.

In **weak**, the little finger moves down the upper arm, possibly inferring lack of muscle. An alternative sign for 'weak' involves the index pointing into the cheek with a twisting movement.

WORST

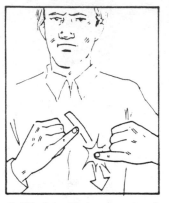

R. little finger tip brushes sharply forward/down against L. little finger tip.

WORSE

R. little finger tip brushes forward/down against L. little finger tip, twice.

SPOIL

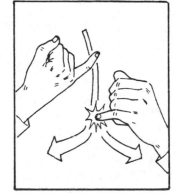

R. little finger moves down sharply to strike L., as both twist to point down.

FAIL

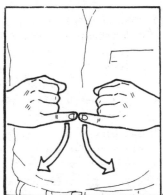

Tips of little fingers touch, then hands twist from wrists so that fingers point down.

ILL

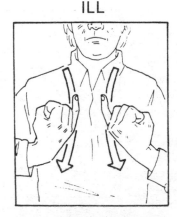

Move both hands simultaneously down chest with little fingers against body.

WEAK

R. little finger moves down left upper arm.

'BAD' HAND SHAPE

The little finger is brought edge down onto the left palm in **wrong**. Like 'right', **wrong** also changes direction in context, so that 'I'm wrong' contacts the signer's chest with this formation, as in the secondary part of **confess**. 'You're wrong', 'She/he's wrong' involves this same hand shape directed towards the person concerned.

A similar message is conveyed by the forward, circular movement in **criticise**, which expresses blame or disapproval being conveyed forward, to another person.

The 'bad' hand formation in **object** links with the negative idea of disapproval, and the sharp, emphatic movement away from the signer adds to the idea of rejection.

The indication of conflict is made evident by the repeated clashing of the little fingers in **fight**.

In **rotten**, the little finger makes a circular movement on the left palm, implying something unsound or of poor quality.

WRONG

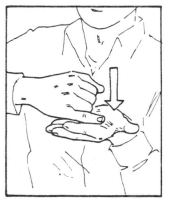

Bring edge of R. little finger sharply down on L. palm.

CONFESS

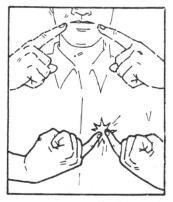

Indexes point to mouth, then move down to closed hands, little fingers extended, contacting left side of chest.

CRITICISE

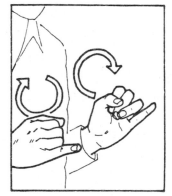

Hands closed, little fingers extended, palms facing, make alternate forward circles with hands.

OBJECT (to)

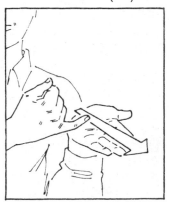

Edge of extended little finger brushes sharply forward/up along L. hand from heel to tips.

FIGHT

Little fingers extended, move up and down banging together several times.

ROTTEN

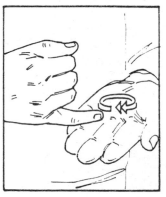

Edge of R. little finger makes circular movement on L. palm.

CLAWED HAND

Signs expressing *tension* or agitation frequently employ a *clawed hand*.

As with other descriptive hand shapes, its location on the head or body, and the specific movement, give further information.

The circular movement on the forehead in **worry** gives an indication of a troubled, anxious mind. Both hands moving alternately can express extreme harassment. An alternative form of this sign involves two clawed hands, palms back, twisting in and down over the eyes.

Moody involves a circular movement in front of the face, suggesting a changeability of attitude, of temper or sullenness, whereas the downward movement in **miserable** seems to imply a long face, a wretched attitude.

The alternating circular movement of the hands in **anxious** implies stomach-churning unease and apprehension.

Hostility connected with affections is shown by the clawed hand drawn across the heart in **jealous**.

An alternative sign involves the bent index finger placed between clenched teeth.

Further examples of clawed hands in emotive signs can be found in Section Four, p. 83.

WORRY

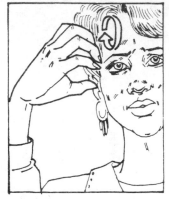

Clawed hand makes circular movement near temple.

SCREAM

Clawed hand, palm back, moves forward/up from mouth.

MOODY

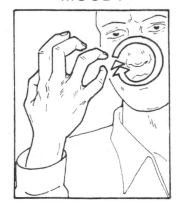

Clawed hand makes circular movement in front of face.

MISERABLE

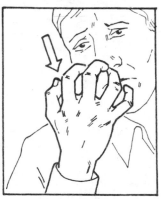

Clawed hand pulls down in front of face.

ANXIOUS

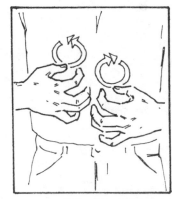

Clawed hands move in alternate circles over the stomach.

JEALOUS

R. clawed hand moves up across chest diagonally left to right, with emphasis.

CLOSED HAND

The *closed hand* is used to indicate *possession*, and changes direction in context, so that the formation is directed palm towards the person or persons concerned. For example, **my** or 'mine' is palm towards the signer as it contacts the chest.

'His/her' involves a closed hand directed palm towards the person referred to, as in **your** illustrated here. In 'your' (plural) and 'their', the closed hand sweeps sideways, palm towards the persons being referred to.

In **whose**, the closed hand follows the sign 'who', which has a number of variations, as illustrated on pp. 38 and 39. It may be signed with the bent index held on the chin, or the tip of the thumb on the chin with the index flexing, or with the index held vertically in front of the body making small circular movements.

The indication of possession can be added after a name, for example 'John's', 'Sue's', 'Mrs Smith's', and so on. Names are usually the finger-spelt initial, the full finger-spelt name, or a person's name sign.

MY

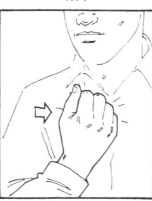

Closed hand moves to contact chest.

YOUR

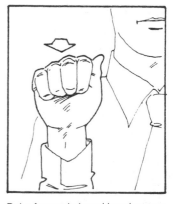

Palm forward closed hand moves towards person or persons concerned.

BELONG

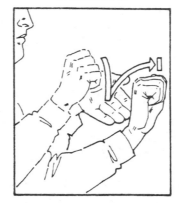

R. closed hand, brought down onto L. flat hand, bounces off and twists forward.

WHOSE

Palm left R. index touches chin, then moves forward, changing to closed hand, palm forward.

MUMMY'S

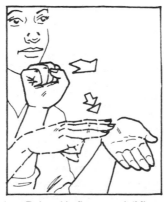

R. hand in finger-spelt 'M' formation taps L. palm twice, then changes to palm forward closed hand with slight forward movement.

SCHOOL'S

Palm forward 'N' hand makes quick side to side downward movement, then changes to palm forward closed hand with slight forward movement.

FLUTTERING FINGERS

Signs that relate to *number* in some form, particularly the questioning of number, frequently involve *fluttering fingers*.

The fluttering fingers in **many** can also indicate 'how many?' when signed with a questioning facial expression.

The location of the fluttering fingers in **when** is the side of the chin where days are indicated. This links the questioning of number and days, implying 'which day?' or 'when?'

The nose is the location for signs relating to age, so the questioning of number in front of the nose indicates 'what age?' or 'how old?'

In **price**, the fluttering fingers move upwards from the left palm — the location of signs relating to money and buying and selling. When used with a questioning facial expression, this sign can be used for 'how much did it cost?' or 'what's the price?'

The downward movement of the fluttering fingers in **count** is an indication of counting down a column of numbers. Sometimes both hands are used to indicate accounting.

The upward and downward movement in **arithmetic** gives more of an indication of calculating, or scoring.

MANY

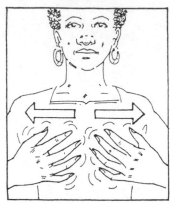

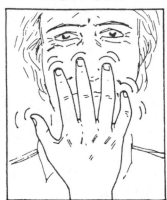

Open hands move apart, fingers fluttering.

WHEN

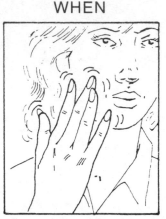

Fingers flutter at side of chin.

HOW OLD

Fingers of open hand flutter in front of nose with questioning facial expression.

PRICE

Fingers of R. hand move up from L. palm and flutter near chin.

COUNT

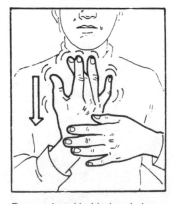

R. open hand behind and above L. moves down with fingers waggling.

ARITHMETIC

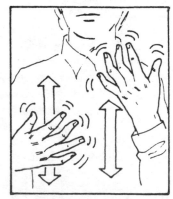

Two open hands move alternately up and down in front of body, fingers fluttering.

SIGN LOCATIONS WITH LINKS TO MEANING

INTRODUCTION

The previous section has looked at several hand shapes and the meaning conveyed by them, with some mention of the location in which the sign is made. It was also pointed out that in Sign Language, information is conveyed by a combination of facial and bodily expression, hand shapes, movement and direction. The location in which the sign takes place is just one of the components involved, but it is useful to look at groups of signs that are made in the same location, in order to understand how these can be linked to meaning.

This section groups signs located on a particular part of the head or body. The first of these is the *forehead* — the mind area. Most signs connected with *mental activity* are made on, or start from, the *forehead*.

Perhaps more obviously, signs connected with looking or sight usually start from the *eye or eyes*, those connected with hearing or sound are usually made near the *ear*, and those concerning speech in its many varieties start from the *mouth*.

Less obviously, signs connected with age are made in front of the *nose*, and days are referred to on the *side of the chin*.

Signs located on the *body*, specifically the chest, usually express affections, desires, personal qualities, emotions, physical feelings and behaviour.

FOREHEAD —
THE MIND AREA

In spoken language we often use figures of speech that make a literal reference to the head in describing thought-related activity. For example, 'he took it into his head', 'it's above my head', 'out of her own head', and many more.

This same literal link exists in signs.

The sign **know** is located on the forehead, using the 'good' hand shape to imply knowledge or understanding.

The phrase 'I'll let you know' is conveyed by the hand moving forward from this position, with the fingers springing open, as if sending information to the person concerned. In 'let me know', the movement is down onto the signer's body as the fingers open.

The index finger points to the forehead in **think** and can be modified to convey 'consider', 'ponder' or 'mull over' and other words or phrases of similar meaning, such as **thoughtful** illustrated here.

The grasping movement of the hand in **remember** seems to convey the idea of holding or keeping something in mind, compared to the way the fingers spring open as if losing something in this version of **forget**.

KNOW

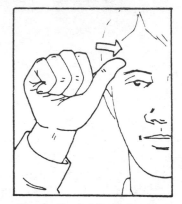

Tip of extended thumb touches side of forehead.

THINK

Index contacts forehead.

THOUGHTFUL

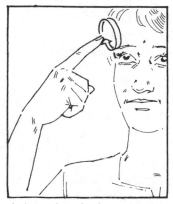

Index makes circular movement on forehead.

REMEMBER

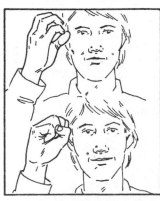

Clawed hand closes sharply to fist at temple.

FORGET

R. full 'O' hand touches temple, then springs open and forward.

FOREHEAD — THE MIND AREA

The positive association of the 'good' hand occurs again in **clever**, where it moves across the forehead to convey mental skill. The movement is also sharp, adding to the idea of a sharp mind.

Like many signs, **clever** can be modified to show degree or intensity. A slightly slower movement and relevant facial expression can convey 'quite clever'. A more emphatic, sharper movement can convey 'very clever' — but again, facial expression is very important in showing this difference.

Wise involves a slower movement of the thumb, in the opposite direction from **clever**.

The idea of understanding, or comprehending, is indicated by the flicking movement of the index in **understand**. In some areas this sign is made by the thumb tip contacting the side of the forehead, then flicking upwards.

An alternative form of the sign **sensible** involves tapping the forehead in exactly the same way as in **silly**, the only difference being that the index is used in **sensible**, and the middle finger in **silly**.

CLEVER

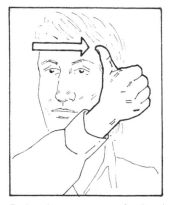

R. thumb moves across forehead in sharp movement.

WISE

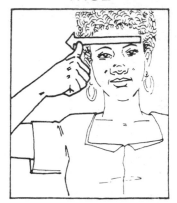

R. thumb moves across forehead, left to right.

UNDERSTAND

Index flicks up at side of forehead.

STUPID

Knuckles of closed hand tap forehead, twice.

SENSIBLE

Index makes small circle on side of forehead, then moves out slightly changing to sign for 'good'.

SILLY

Tap forehead twice, with middle finger.

FOREHEAD: IMAGINATIVE THOUGHTS

When we express various forms of abstract or inventive thoughts in English, we often use figures of speech that imply that our thoughts are reaching out in some way, such as 'I was miles away', or 'a stretch of the imagination'.

Signs expressing abstract thoughts also seem to suggest this reaching out, by movement away from the forehead, possibly to suggest that the thought is imaginative and not a concrete experience.

Imagine and **dream** start on the forehead and move in a circular motion, moving out from the head as if to emphasise the abstract nature of the thoughts. A full flat hand is also sometimes used.

The implication of creative or imaginative ideas, as in **suppose**, **guess** and **idea**, is similarly shown here by the outward movement of the index, away from the forehead.

IMAGINE

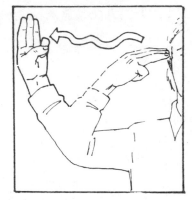

'M' hand touches temple, then moves out with slight waggling movement.

DREAM

Tips of R. 'M' hand contact forehead, then hand moves out in small arcs, eyes closed for emphasis.

SUPPOSE

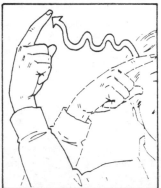

Index moves out from forehead with slight waggling movement.

GUESS

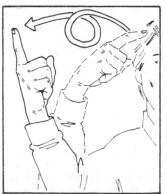

R. index moves away from head in looping movement.

IDEA

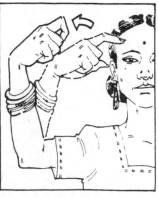

Index points to temple, then pulls out and bends.

FOREHEAD: COMPOUND SIGNS

Compound signs are those that combine more than one sign, or parts of signs. All the compound signs in this group are connected with mental activity, and start from the forehead. The secondary part of each sign gives more specific information to clarify that thought activity further.

The implication of belief is made here by combining 'think' and 'true' in the sign **believe**. This sign is also sometimes made with a combination of 'know' and 'true'.

The secondary part of **decide** involves a sharp and decisive movement appropriate to its meaning, which also occurs in 'rule' and 'law' (p. 72) and in this version of **estimate**, implying a judgement made after a considered calculation.

This contrasts with the indecision and uncertainty conveyed by the weighing movement of the hands in **doubt**.

The idea of mixed or disordered thoughts is expressed in **confuse** by combining 'think' and 'complicated'.

The secondary part of **experience** possibly indicates an imaginary sheet of events, indicating experience or knowledge of those areas.

BELIEVE

R. index points to forehead then moves down to finish with blade of flat hand on L. palm.

DECIDE/DECISION

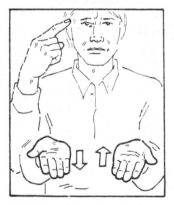

R. index touches forehead, then moves down sharply onto L. palm, with one tap for decide, two taps for decision.

ESTIMATE

R. index makes circular movement on temple, then moves down sharply onto L. palm.

DOUBT

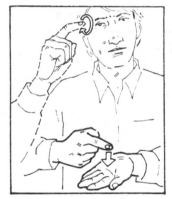

R. index points to temple, then both hands, palms up, move up and down alternately.

CONFUSE

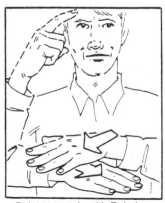

Point to temple with R. index, then two open hands cross sharply.

EXPERIENCE

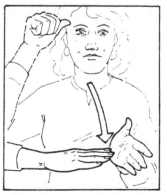

R. thumb touches temple, moves down changing to flat hand and brushes down across L. palm.

FOREHEAD: BUNCHED HANDS

In this last group of signs connected with mental activity, bunched hands are used to give an effective visual image of gathering or passing on knowledge or information.

In **take in**, the hand starts open, and draws back closing to a bunched hand, as if the information is being absorbed, and taken in mentally. In **learn**, the bunched hands move alternately to the temples.

Teach and **remind** must both change direction in context to make correct visual sense, so that the movement is towards the person concerned. For example, 'I was taught' or 'teach me' would involve the bunched hands moving from the temples and twisting to point and move back towards the signer.

Similarly, 'remind him/her' or 'remind you' both move towards the relevant person. For 'remind me', the bunched hand contacts the signer's shoulder.

TAKE IN (absorb)

Flat hand, with fingers and thumb pointing forward, moves back to temple as fingers close onto thumb.

LEARN

Bunched hands move up alternately to temples.

TEACH

Bunched hands point to temples, then twist forward and make two short forward movements.

REMIND

Bunched hand contacts temple, then moves towards person concerned as if tapping him or her. For 'remind me' move from temple to tap on shoulder.

EYE OR EYES

Signs connected with looking, or *sight*, usually start from the *eye or eyes*.

Find is often made with the upward grasping movement alone, and does not always start from the eye.

There are several signs for **search**; the sign illustrated here gives the indication of trying to find, or looking for something.

An alternative sign for **look after** starts with the index moving from the eye, followed by the sign 'keep' (not illustrated).

Blind may be signed with both hands in the 'N' hand shape starting at the inner corners of the eyes and moving outwards, or the same movement with flat hands, indicating closure, as in 'private' (p. 74) and some variations in the sign for 'deaf'.

SEE

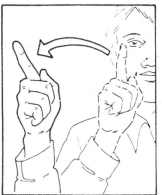

Index moves forward from eye.

FIND

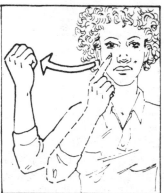

Index points to eye, then moves away, and grasps upwards to fist sharply as if finding something.

SEARCH

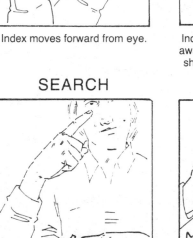

R. index moves from eye to contact L. in repeated forward brushing movement, as formation moves sideways, fingers slightly bent.

SHOW

Flat hands palm back, held under eyes, sweep forward/down and apart.

LOOK AFTER

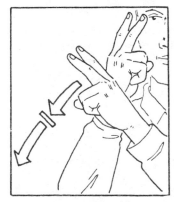

Two 'V' hands, blade of R. on top of L.; formation moves down from eye in two movements.

BLIND

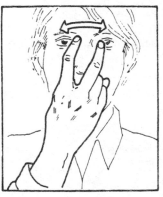

R. 'V' hand, fingers slightly bent, held in front of eyes, moves from side to side twice.

EYE OR EYES

In the signs **look** and **read**, the movement of the 'V' hand represents the path of the *eye gaze*, or the direction in which the eyes are looking. It is therefore possible to convey much additional information relevant to particular contexts.

For example, in 'look around', 'look up and down', 'look at the blackboard', etc., the movement is appropriate to that context, accompanied by movement of the eyes in the same direction.

A 'V' hand held away from the body, with the fingers pointing back to the signer, indicates another person looking at the signer, as in 'she looked at me', for example.

Both hands held forward, with all the fingers pointing back to the signer, can indicate a lot of people looking at the signer, as in 'everyone was looking at me'.

Two 'V' hands held away from the body, with the fingers pointing towards each other, can convey two people looking at each other.

In **read**, the sweeping movement of the 'V' hand represents the movement of the eyes in reading, and the direction and type of movement is again appropriate to the context. In the context of reading a poster on a wall, for example, the sideways sweeping movement would be made in the appropriate direction. Reading a telephone directory would involve an upward and downward sweep, relevant to reading up and down columns of words or numbers, and so on.

Like many other signs, both **look** and **read** can be further modified, both in the way the sign is made and by facial and bodily expression, to convey a quick glance, looking at for a long time, or reading over and over again, and so on.

There are many other variations, and these are just some examples to illustrate the basic idea. The accompanying movement of the eyes is particularly important in these signs.

LOOK

'V' hand moves from eye, forward, or towards the person or thing concerned.

READ

R. 'V' hand moves from eye to sweep twice along L. palm.

EAR

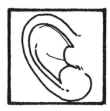

Signs connected with hearing or *sound* are usually made near the *ear*.

The illustrated sign for **hearing** incorporates the 'good' hand moving from ear to mouth. This indicates a hearing person. An alternative sign commonly used by the Deaf Community involves the same movement with the index finger, or a forward, repeated movement of the index from below the mouth, indicating a speaking person.

The configuration used in **deaf** also sometimes moves to the mouth, indicating no hearing and no speech, although this is now less commonly used.

A flat hand may variably be used, implying closure, found also in 'private' (p. 74) and some variations of 'blind'.

HEAR

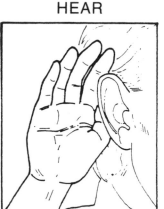

Slightly cupped hand behind ear.

LISTEN

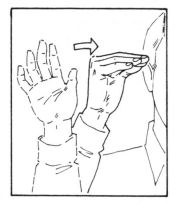

Hand closes sharply to bunched hand, at ear.

HEARING

Closed hand, thumb extended, moves from ear to mouth.

DEAF

'N' hand pointing up, palm left, touches ear.

NOISE

Index makes circular movements around ear.

IGNORE

Indexes point to ears, then flick sharply down and to one side, simultaneously.

MOUTH

Signs connected with *speech* usually start from the *mouth*.

Very often the index finger or fingers move from the mouth to express speech and spoken terms in a wide variety of forms.

SPEAK

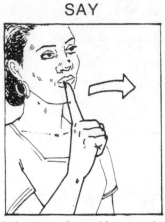

Index makes short repeated movements backwards and forwards from mouth.

SAY

Index moves forward from mouth.

ORDER (command)

Index points to mouth, then moves sharply to point forward.

REPLY

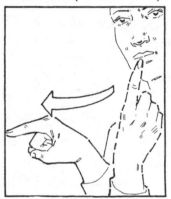

Indexes extended, R. on lips, L. held slightly forward. Hands twist sharply to reverse positions.

REPORT

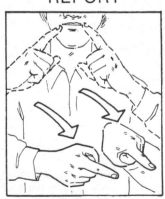

Indexes touch sides of mouth, then move forward/left.

TALK

Closed hands, indexes extended. R. hand points to mouth, then bangs top of L. hand twice, at right angles.

ANNOUNCE

Index fingers touch sides of mouth, then sweep forward and apart.

MOUTH:
CONVEYING INFORMATION

All the signs illustrated on this page can be used to express the conveying of information in the sense of relating a story, telling a tale, or giving an account. For convenience, each sign has been given an equivalent English word which reflects the more common specific meaning of each, but any of these could be used in the sense of 'let me tell you about it'.

Context, or more often personal preference, may determine the choice of any of these signs. More than one may occur in the same conversation to add variety and interest.

Information and **explain** both change direction in context. Both are drawn with the sign moving forward from the signer, which would be appropriate for contexts such as 'for your information' or 'I'll explain'.

In different contexts, such as 'I need information' or 'explain what happened', the hands would rotate backwards, towards the signer.

TALE

R. index moves down from mouth, changing to flat hand, and brushes down index edge of L. flat hand.

DESCRIBE

R. index points to lips, moves down to flat hand above L. Hands move in alternate horizontal circles.

STORY

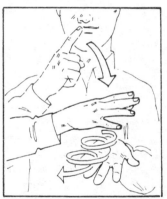

R. index points to mouth, moves down changing to open hand, and makes two forward circular movements along L. open hand.

INFORMATION

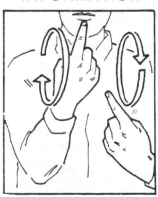

Palm back closed hands, indexes extended, move in forward alternating circles from the mouth.

EXPLAIN

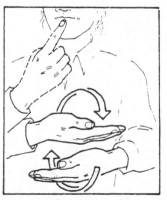

R. index touches mouth, then two flat hands rotate round each other in forward circles.

MOUTH:
COMPOUND SIGNS

The compound signs in this group have meanings connected with spoken terms, and start from the mouth.

The implication of a pledge or assurance is made by combining 'say' and 'true' in the sign **promise**.

The secondary part of **confess** involves both hands in the 'bad' hand shape, contacting the signer's body indicating 'I'm wrong' or 'guilty'. This meaning is preceded by the indication of a spoken term to imply acknowledgement or statement of guilt.

The downward, brushing movement of the hand in the secondary part of **polite** occurs also in 'behave', 'patient', and 'accept' (p. 84). This seems to be a submissive gesture, as if pushing down or controlling the emotions, and is used here to express the controlled refinement of politeness.

In **law**, the index moves down from the mouth to contact the left palm in a decisive movement appropriate to the idea of rules set down by authority.

PROMISE

R. index points to mouth, then blade of R. flat hand hits L. palm with emphasis.

CONFESS

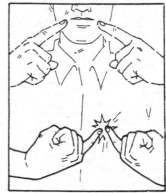

Indexes point to mouth, then move down to closed hands, little fingers extended, contacting left side of chest.

POLITE

Index touches mouth, changes to flat hand and brushes down body once.

LAW

Index moves from mouth to contact L. palm with emphasis.

MOUTH:
DESCRIPTIVE HAND SHAPES

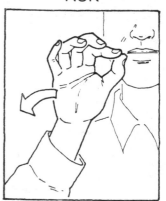

R. 'O' palm forward moves forward from side of mouth in small arc.

The hand shape in **ask** and **answer** occurs in signs related to questions and answers. In 'question' (not illustrated), this hand shape moves in the shape of a question mark in the air. The hand shape is derived from the old finger-spelt letter 'Q', of the British manual alphabet.

Like many other signs, **ask** changes direction in context — for example:

'Ask me' — the hand shape moves towards and contacts the signer's body.
'Ask him/her' — the hand shape moves towards the person concerned.
'Ask everyone' — the hand shape sweeps round in a horizontal circle.

In this version of **answer**, the same hand shape moves back towards the mouth after contacting the tip of the left thumb, the location of the finger-spelt letter 'A'. One sign for 'interview' (not illustrated) can be made by repeated contact, in a circular movement, of this same right hand configuration against the tip of the left thumb, indicating questions and answers.

The opening and closing movements of the fingers onto the thumbs in **conversation** and **gossip** is a representation of the mouth opening and closing in talking. This same movement can be made with just one hand, held in front of the mouth to mean 'talk'.

Both hands opening and closing, moving in horizontal circles, can indicate a lot of chatter, or discussion.

ANSWER

L. hand thumb up; R. 'O' hand contacts tip of L. thumb and moves to mouth.

CONVERSATION

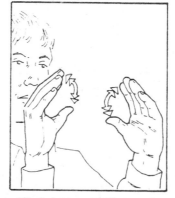

Hands face each other, one in front of mouth, one held forward. Fingers open and close onto thumbs to indicate people talking.

GOSSIP

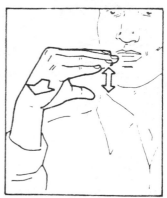

Fingers open and close onto thumb whilst moving forward from mouth.

MOUTH:
DESCRIPTIVE HAND SHAPES

Other hand shapes are also used to illustrate vocal sounds in a visual way, as in **sing**, **scream** and **shout**.

'N' hands circle alternately upwards from mouth.

SCREAM

SHOUT

Scream employs a clawed hand which is very common in signs indicating tension or stress.

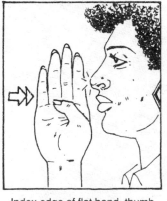

Clawed hand, palm back, moves forward/up from mouth.

Closed hand, palm forward, in front of mouth, moves forward springing sharply open.

PRIVATE

SECRET

The flat hand or hands held against the mouth in **private** and **secret** give the idea of closure, of nothing passing the lips.

Index edge of flat hand, thumb tucked in, taps nose twice.

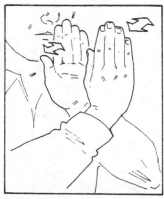

Flat hands, edge to edge against each other, in front of mouth, move in very small alternate side to side movements.

MOUTH:
NUMBER INCORPORATION

In referring to amounts of money, pounds can be expressed by the appropriate number of fingers moving forward from the mouth, for amounts up to £10.

To express a figure such as £3.50 illustrated here, the hand moves forward from the mouth in the configuration for £3, with the 50 signed in the forward position. The 50 shown in the illustration is a variation used in the North East of England.

For amounts over £10, the number is signed in neutral space, then the index moves forward from the lips, to indicate £.

Further descriptions of signs involving number incorporation can be found on p. 96 and in Section Six.

£1

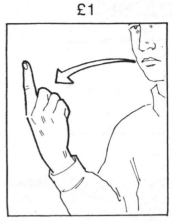

Index finger moves forward from the mouth.

£2

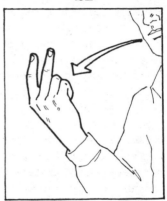

Index and middle fingers move forward from the mouth.

£3.50

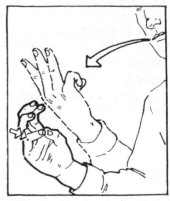

Three fingers move forward from the mouth, then the sign for 50 is made in the forward position.

NOSE

Signs connected with *age* are made on, or start from the *nose*.

The fluttering fingers in **age** are located in front of the nose and give an indication of number in relation to age. When this sign is made with a questioning facial expression, it implies 'what age?' or 'how old?'

As illustrated here, when age is given, the hand moves forward from the nose in the relevant configuration for the number of years being indicated.

Six and **sixteen** shown here are variations used in the North East of England. Other areas use different number systems, but the principle of the number moving forward from the nose is still used.

For ages over 20, the hand moves forward from the nose in the configuration of the first digit in the number, with the second digit signed in the forward position. So, for example, '35 years old' would start with three fingers moving forward from the nose, changing to five in the forward position, and so on.

OLD

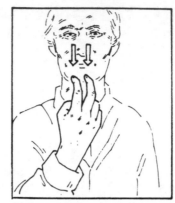

Fingers of 'V' hand pull down and bend in front of nose.

YOUNG

R. index, middle finger and thumb extended, move slightly forward, closing fingers onto thumb, in front of nose.

AGE

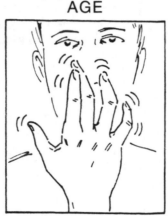

Fingers of open hand flutter in front of nose.

FIVE (yrs old)

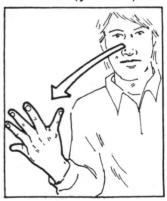

Palm back open hand moves forward from in front of nose.

SIX (yrs old)

Little finger extended, hand moves forward from in front of nose.

SIXTEEN (yrs old)

Little finger extended, hand moves forward from in front of the nose and bends repeatedly.

NOSE

Signs connected with falseness and pretence also occur on the nose.

The illustrated sign **false** is also used to mean 'imitation' and in some areas also means 'pretend' and 'deceive'.

FALSE

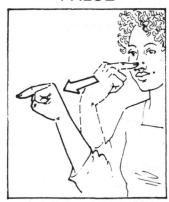

Middle finger extended, touches nose, then hand moves forward whilst twisting to point forward.

PRETEND

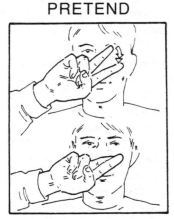

Middle finger of 'V' hand brushes down nose, closing behind index twice quickly.

JOKE

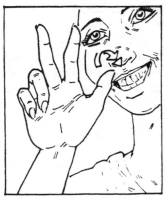

Index, middle and thumb extended, move in small circles, thumbtip brushing nose.

SIDE OF CHIN

Days are usually indicated at the *side of the chin*.

This version of **date** is very similar to 'number' in which a closed hand taps the front of the chin. However, **date** is located at the side of the chin, to link 'number' and days, thus indicating date.

The fluttering fingers in **when** give an indication of questioning in relation to number, and again the location at the side of the chin gives the further link to days, thus implying 'what day?' or 'when?'

The forward movement of the index in **tomorrow** indicates one day in the future, two fingers moving forward would indicate 'in two days', and so on. In some areas 'next week' is indicated by the hand in the configuration for '7' moving forward, from the side of the chin. A backward movement of this configuration indicates 'last week'.

The index moves backward in **yesterday**, indicating one day past. 'Two days ago' involves two fingers moving backwards, and so on.

More details of expressing future and past can be found in Section Six.

DAY

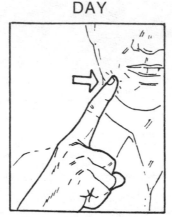

R. closed hand, index finger extended, touches side of face.

EVERY DAY

Backs of fingers stroke forwards on side of face, then index touches side of face.

DATE

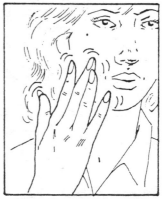

Closed hand palm left knocks against side of chin twice.

WHEN

Fingers flutter at side of chin.

TOMORROW

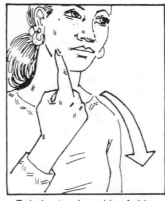

R. index touches side of chin, then hand swings forward/down, finishing palm up.

YESTERDAY

R. index held on side of chin, drops down/back.

BODY: AFFECTIONS AND DESIRES

The bosom, or breast, of a human being is the imagined seat of the passions and feelings.

The *body*, specifically the chest, is most frequently the location for signs expressing affections, desires, *physical and emotional feelings*, and behaviour.

The sign **feel** involves the tips of the middle fingers moving up the body, to convey feeling in both the physical and emotional senses.

The connection of the heart with affections is perhaps an obvious link.

Like, **love** and **hate**, although not made directly on the heart, are made on the upper chest, and have this link to meaning. **Want** and **need** are similarly located, expressing needs and desires.

FEEL

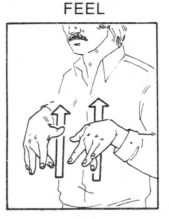

Tips of middle fingers brush up body from waist to upper trunk.

LOVE

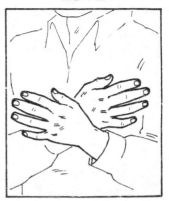

Hands crossed at wrists, held on chest.

LIKE (prefer)

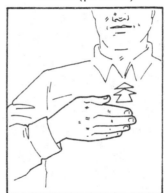

Flat hand taps chest twice.

HATE

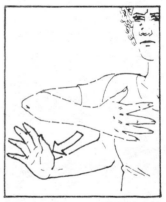

Open hand on upper chest twists to palm forward and pushes away from body with distaste.

WANT

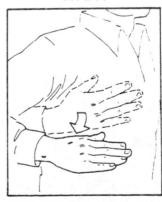

Flat hand on side of upper chest brushes down, twisting to palm down in small movement.

NEED

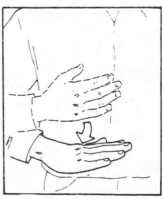

R. flat hand, held on right side above waist, brushes down, twisting to palm down.

BODY: DISPOSITIONS

Signs expressing *natural inclinations* or personal qualities are also located on the body.

Again there are connections with the heart in the location of these signs. The idea of kind-heartedness is expressed in **kind** and **generous**, with the 'good' hand shapes moving forward from the heart.

This hand shape occurs again to express bravery and courage, when the hands move forward from the body changing from flat hands in **brave** and **courage** (also used for 'confident').

Another common variation of **confident** is this initialised sign, in which the 'C' hand is located over the heart. Losing confidence can be shown very descriptively by this 'C' formation moving *down* the body.

The 'good' hand shapes appear again in **proud**, circling backwards onto the signer's body to indicate the personal feeling of self-esteem.

KIND (good)

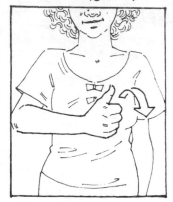

Closed hand, thumb up over heart, moves forward with slight twist.

GENEROUS

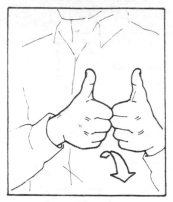

Closed hands, thumbs extended, held together over heart, move forward in small arc.

BRAVE

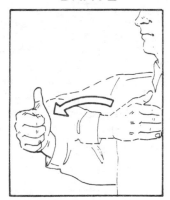

R. flat hand on chest, moves forward to closed hand thumb extended in sharp movement.

COURAGE

Contact trunk with fingertips, then move hands forward closing sharply to closed hands, thumbs extended.

CONFIDENT

R. 'C' hand taps twice against chest over the heart.

PROUD

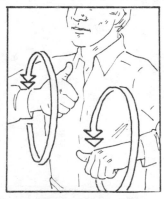

Thumbs brush down chest in alternate backward circles.

BODY:
PHYSICAL FEELINGS

Move hand round in circle on stomach.

The *physical* sensation of hunger is aptly expressed on the area of the stomach. The illustration here for **hungry** is one variation of this sign; others include the same circular movement made with a closed hand, or two closed hands, moving down in one short movement over the stomach area.

The short, downward brushing movement in **satisfied** seems to imply fullness, although its use can express satisfaction or contentment in any sense.

There are other signs to express illness, but the illustration here for **ill** is commonly used, in which the 'bad' hand shapes move down the body. A natural opposite to this, i.e. **well**, incorporates the 'good' hand shapes in contact with the body.

In **tired** the hands flop or droop downwards in a way that reflects the weariness of the body. This movement may be modulated to show degree or intensity to express 'quite tired', 'exhausted' and so on.

SATISFIED

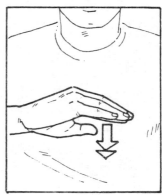

Index edge of slightly cupped hand brushes down chest, twice.

ILL

Move both hands simultaneously down chest with little fingers against body.

WELL

Thumbs move down upper chest, then twist forward.

TIRED

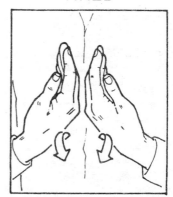

Tips of palm back bent hands on upper chest. Hands twist down so that blades contact chest.

BODY: EMOTIONS

The chest area is again the location for signs expressing *emotional feelings*. **Pleased**, illustrated here with the flat hand rubbing in a circular movement on the chest, is used in some areas to mean 'sorry'. In spite of the contrary meanings involved, it should be remembered that signs do not occur in isolation: context and facial expression should avoid any confusion. The sign illustrated as **sorry** uses the same movement with a closed hand and is sometimes made with the little finger extended.

The *upward* brushing movement of the hand on the upper chest in **upset** possibly indicates the emotions coming up to the surface. This seems to be appropriate to the idea of discontent and distress, and contrasts with the *downward* brushing movement in 'satisfied' on the previous page.

The emphatic downward movement in **depressed** appears to be a clear statement of a depressed, down-hearted condition. The index finger here represents the person, the 'self', being pressed down.

The same movement of the right hand alone occurs in **dejected**, and is used to convey a variety of related meanings, such as sad, dispirited, discouraged, crestfallen, and so on, depending on context.

In other contexts, and with appropriate facial expression, it is also used as an expression of relief, or of calming down.

PLEASED

Flat hand rubs in circular movement on chest.

SORRY

Closed hand rubs in circular movement on chest.

UPSET

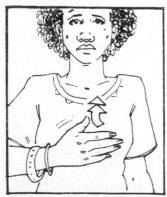

Flat hand brushes up/forward, twice, on chest, in small movement.

DEPRESSED

L. flat hand, on top of R. index; hold in against body, move formation down with stress.

DEJECTED

Index edge of palm down flat hand brushes emphatically down chest in one movement.

BODY: AGITATED EMOTIONS

Clawed hands frequently occur in signs indicating tension, or *agitation*.

The upward clawing movement of the hands in **angry** seems to indicate the emotions boiling up within the body. This sign can express 'mad', 'cross', 'furious' and so on, by the degree of intensity with which it is signed, by appropriate facial and bodily expression, and by lip pattern.

The sign is sometimes made with the clawed hands moving up in one emphatic movement, ending with the palms facing upwards.

A clawed hand again helps to convey the tension inherent in **complain** and the upward movement adds to the idea of discontent and dissatisfaction (another contrast to the downward movement of 'satisfied', p. 81).

Exciting and **frightened** both use clawed hands, but the quick movement of agitation in **exciting** and the quivering, trembling movement in **frightened** (with appropriate expression) show quite different meanings.

Hostility connected with affections is shown by the clawed hand drawn across the heart in this version of **jealous**.

In **keen** the hands are not fully clawed, but the movement is agitated and conveys the idea of stimulation, enthusiasm and eagerness.

ANGRY

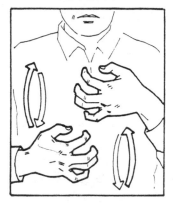

Clawed hands alternately claw up body several times.

COMPLAIN

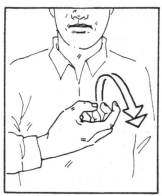

R. clawed hand, palm up, brushes up chest several times.

EXCITING

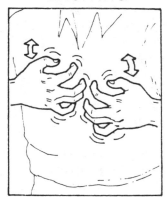

Rub clawed hands up and down on chest alternately in quick movements.

FRIGHTENED

Two clawed hands R. above L. quiver into body.

JEALOUS

R. clawed hand moves up across chest diagonally left to right, with emphasis.

KEEN

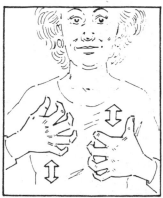

Fingers bent at second knuckles; hands rub up and down alternately, on chest, in short, quick movements.

BODY: BEHAVIOUR

The last group of signs located on the body includes those indicating conduct and *behaviour*.

The signs illustrated here all involve a downward, brushing movement of one or both hands. Although only a subjective view, this seems to be a submissive gesture, as if pushing down, suppressing, or controlling the emotions.

There is a contrast here to the upward movement in signs that express the emotions rising, as in 'upset' (p. 82) and 'angry' and 'complain' shown on p. 83.

In **patient**, both hands make this downward brushing movement alternately. As with many other signs, **patient** is only one word equivalent to the meaning of this sign. Depending on context, it can be used to express tolerance, endurance, perseverence or submission.

Accept is very similar in meaning, and depending on context, can be used to express such ideas as 'receive with resignation or passivity', 'I had to accept it', 'on sufferance' and so on.

BEHAVE

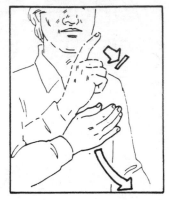

Raise R. index and move forward slightly; change to flat hand and brush down body.

PATIENT (calm)

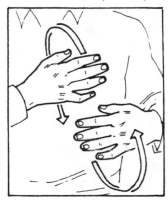

Flat hands brush alternately down body in backward circular movement.

ACCEPT

Head held down; tips of flat hand contact chin, then hand brushes down body in small movement.

Section Five

REPRESENTATIVE HAND SHAPES

INTRODUCTION

A significant feature of sign language is the specific way deaf people use certain hand shapes as a direct *representation* of people and things.

These hand shapes occur in a wide variety of signs, but this section looks at their specific use in context to represent *people* and *vehicles*.

The index finger can be used to signify a *person*. That is not to say that the index is the 'sign' for person, but that it can be used to directly represent a person, as if it 'becomes' the person. In this way it can be used to show location, movement and position in relation to other people or things.

It can come and go, move backwards, forwards, towards, away from, be in front of, or follow. The possibilities are endless and signs based on this principle give just a glimpse of the many shades of meaning it can express.

In the same way, all the fingers can be used to represent *people*. This can mean a group of people, a queue, a line of people, a crowd, and so on. The fingers can again show location and movements in an infinite number of ways.

The inverted 'V' hand is commonly used as a direct representation of *legs*. In this way, a change in perspective can be given to show a closer, more detailed description of the movements of an individual.

The specific movements of the *head* can be reinforced and emphasised by the representative movements of a closed hand. This again gives a closer, more detailed perspective of an individual's movements.

Vehicles are very commonly represented by the flat hand. Just as with the other representative hand shapes in this section, the hand 'becomes' the vehicle and can depict movement, direction and speed.

PEOPLE

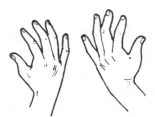

LEGS

HEAD

VEHICLE

INDEX FINGER: PERSON

The signs illustrated on this page show the use of the *index finger* as a direct representation of a *person*.

In **self** as illustrated, the index contacts the signer's body to indicate I or me in person — 'myself'. 'Yourself', 'herself', 'himself', etc., involve this repeated short downwards movement of the index palm towards the signer, but held forward, away from the body towards the person or persons concerned.

The repeated sideways movement in **each** indicates individual people.

Alone involves the index moving down, behind the left palm, to signify a solitary figure. The sideways movement seems to emphasise the singularity of the individual.

The first part of the movement in **lonely** gives this same indication of isolation, with the final movement suggesting a forlorn, forsaken figure. The secondary part of this sign, with the open hands pointing down, is also used on its own to convey boredom, of being at a loss or a loose end.

In **depressed**, the index again represents a person, the 'self' being pressed down.

The raised index in **boss** is possibly an indication of someone high up and in authority.

SELF

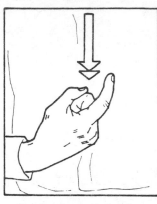

Brush extended index down body, twice, or towards person concerned.

EACH

R. closed hand, index extended, moves from left to right in three hops.

ALONE

L. hand palm back, R. index extended, placed above/behind L; R. moves down then to the right.

LONELY

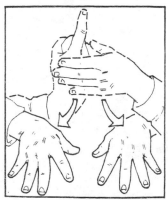

R. index pointing up moves down behind L. hand, then both hands open and swing to point down.

DEPRESSED

L. flat hand, on top of R. index; hold in against body, move formation down with stress.

BOSS

Index held up at side of head with slight movement. Both hands may be used.

INDEX FINGER: PERSON

The circling movement of the index in **someone** shows an indefinite indication of a person and is also used in question form to mean 'who' (p. 38).

Anyone involves the sign 'any' and the index, representing an individual, being signed simultaneously, to indicate any single person.

The simple movements of coming and going are indicated by the index in **come** and **go**.

Escape is only one word equivalent to this sign's meaning. It can be used to indicate leaving in any sense, but the sharp movement is very descriptive of a person leaving in haste. The index passes under the left hand, adding to the idea of evasion, or of slipping away. Depending on context, it can also mean leaving abruptly, before the end, or without waiting.

The idea of sneaking off, or leaving without permission, can be reinforced by making the sign at the side of the body.

Both indexes are used in **follow**, as an indication of one person following another.

SOMEONE

Extended index, pointing up, palm back, moves in small horizontal circles.

ANYONE

L. index pointing up, held stationary; R. hand, thumb and little finger extended, sweeps across front of body in waggling movement.

COME

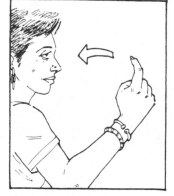

R. closed hand, index extended, held away from body, moves back towards body.

GO

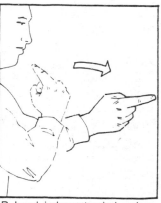

R. hand, index extended, swings forward and points away from body.

ESCAPE

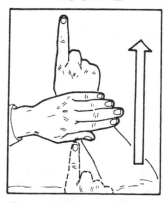

R. hand, index extended, passes under L. hand in sharp movement.

FOLLOW

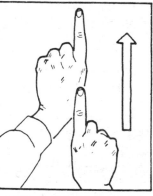

Indexes pointing forward, R. behind L., move formation forward.

INDEX FINGER: PERSON

The use of *both indexes* to represent *two people*, can illustrate movement and position in relation to each other.

This is clearly indicated in **meet**, where the indexes move in to meet each other, and in **approach**, where one index moves towards the other.

The position of one person in relation to another is indicated by the side-by-side position of the fingers in **beside**.

In a more abstract sense, the indication of contrasting interests or diametrically opposing views is conveyed by the separating movement in **oppose**.

The sharp movement of the index fingers towards each other in **against** and **competition** gives an indication of rivalry, of individuals coming together in a competitive way. The idea of conflict can be accentuated by the indexes moving up and down alternately, still pointing towards each other.

If it is remembered that each index finger can be used to represent a person, it is possible to convey information such as, 'She came in and stood in front of me', 'He met me and we went together', 'I met many different people', and so on. The information can be conveyed by the appropriate movements of the index fingers alone.

MEET

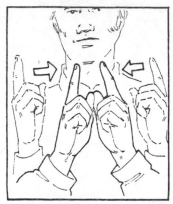

Indexes, held apart, move in to meet each other.

APPROACH

L. index held away from body; R. index moves from near body towards L.

BESIDE

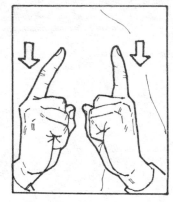

Two closed hands, indexes extended, held at side of body, make slight downward movement.

OPPOSE

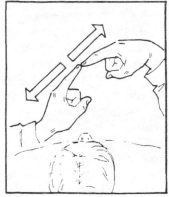

Indexes point towards each other, held diagonally in front of body, then pull apart.

AGAINST (vs.)

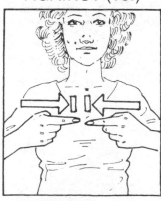

Two closed hands, indexes extended 6" apart, move towards each other in sharp movement.

COMPETITION

Indexes jerk towards each other several times whilst moving down.

THE FINGERS: PEOPLE

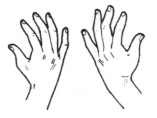

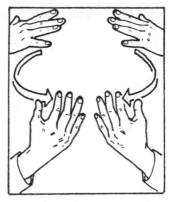

Open hands, palm down, pointing in at sides of head, swing out and twist to point back.

INTEGRATE

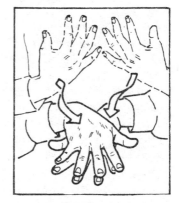

Open hands, palms back, move forward whilst twisting to palm down, R. on top of L., in one smooth movement.

Just as the index finger can be used to represent an individual person, and show movement and position in relation to other people and things, so all *the fingers* can be used to represent *people* with their relative positions and movements.

The fingers in **crowd** indicate a gathering of people, such as an audience, group or class.

Integrate implies separate sets of people coming together in a unified way.

The sharp movement towards each other of all the fingers in **war** is the same as the movement of the index fingers in 'against' (p. 90). In **war**, the fingers represent people coming together in rivalry or conflict, just as individuals are represented in 'against'.

The indication of people moving in a line can be made by moving both hands, as in the illustration **line of people.** This is just one example of the many, many ways that the fingers can be used to show the position and movement of people in different contexts.

LINE OF PEOPLE

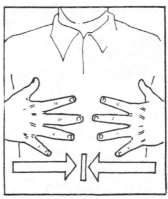

Hands move forward, one in front of the other.

WAR

Open hands move sharply towards each other, and stop abruptly.

INVERTED 'V' HAND: LEGS

This hand shape is commonly used as a direct representation of *legs*. In context it can illustrate specific detail, in a visually appropriate way, giving a closer, more detailed perspective of an individual's position and movements than is possible with the index finger alone. As with the other representative hand shapes, the information that can be conveyed in context is without limit. The signs based on this principle give just a sample of the possibilities.

Stand can be located in space to indicate an individual's position in relation to other people and things.

The sign **fall** in its base form, as illustrated, represents the simple action of a person falling over. Falling in different contexts would each be signed differently. For example, falling down stairs, falling from a height, or falling down a hole would all be signed in a way that directly represented the action involved in the specific context.

It should be noted that this hand shape would not be used to describe an object, such as a tree, falling over: it represents a person, or more specifically the action of the legs.

STAIRS

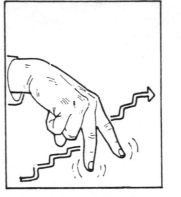

Fingers mime walking on stairs — upwards for 'upstairs', downwards for 'downstairs'.

RIDE

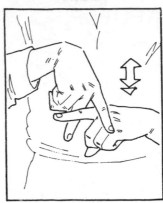

R. 'V' hand on L. index finger. Formation moves up and down to indicate riding.

STAND

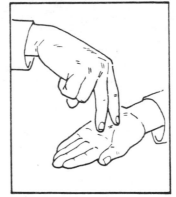

R. 'V' hand stands on L. palm.

DRUNK

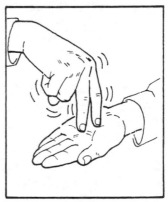

Tips of R. 'V' hand contact L. palm, R. hand rotates slightly.

FALL

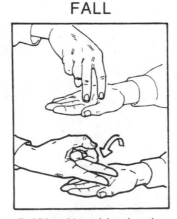

R. 'V' hand 'stands' on L. palm, then falls over to finish palm up on L. palm.

KNEEL

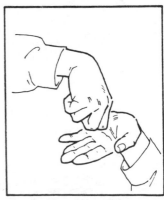

R. index and middle finger, bent at 2nd knuckles, placed on L. palm.

INVERTED 'V' HAND: LEGS

Jump is also illustrated in its base form, indicating jumping up and down. Other contexts, such as jumping over something, or jumping onto or off something, would be signed differently, in a visually appropriate way.

The indication of a person lying down is given in **lie** and the repeated turning of the 'V' hand in **toss and turn** gives a clear indication of a restless figure, unable to sleep.

In **travel** and **tour**, the fingers are bent slightly and flex rather than 'walk'. This also occurs in some variations of the sign 'walk' (p. 35) and is another way of indicating the repeated movement of the legs.

JUMP

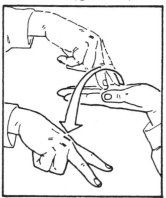

R. index and middle on palm of L. 'jump' up, bend and land back on palm.

OFF (get off)

Tips of 'V' hand stand on L. palm, then move off in small arc.

LIE (down)

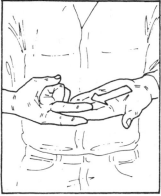

Palm of R. 'V' hand makes small movement along L. palm.

TOSS and TURN

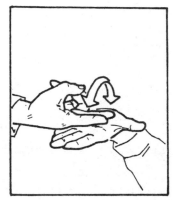

R. 'V' hand twists from palm up to palm down in repeated contact with L. palm.

TRAVEL

'V' hand, fingers slightly bent, moves forward twisting from side to side.

TOUR

Fingers of 'V' hand, slightly bent, move round in horizontal circle with slight flexing.

CLOSED HAND: HEAD

The *closed hand* or fist can be used to represent a round or solid object. In the signs illustrated here, it represents the movement of the *head*, and is used to reinforce accompanying head movement.

This gives an even closer, more detailed perspective of a person's movements and adds emphasis to specific details of how the head moves in different contexts.

No and **refuse** represent shaking one's head in disagreement.

Nodding the head in consent is emphasised by the nodding hand in **yes**. **Yes 1** represents the signer nodding, and **yes 2** represents someone nodding to the signer.

This sign can be modified to indicate nodding in agreement when one disagrees but doesn't want to argue, or when one hasn't understood. The signer's head is turned away in a derisory, uninterested manner, and the hand and head nod, as if saying 'yes, yes, yes'. This also applies to **yes 2**, when describing somebody nodding to the signer.

The last examples show the head represented literally in **duck**, where it 'ducks' down behind the left hand, and figuratively in **loss of face** where it represents hiding one's head in shame.

NO (~ yes)

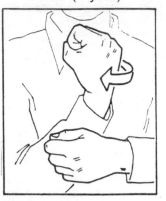

Right forearm rests on L. closed hand; R. fist twists sharply from palm back to palm forward.

REFUSE

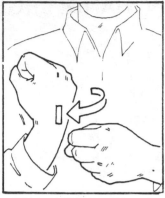

Palm back R. fist, resting on L. fist, twists sharply to palm forward.

YES 1

R. closed hand, supported by L. index, twists from palm forward to palm down, like a head nodding.

YES 2

Palm back closed R. hand 'nods' towards signer.

DUCK (to)

R. fist 'ducks' down behind L. flat hand, to emphasise the simultaneous head movement.

LOSS OF FACE

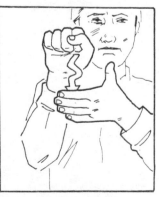

R. fist moves down behind L. flat hand in side to side wavering movement.

FLAT HAND: VEHICLE

The signs illustrated on this page show the *flat hand* or hands being used as a direct representation of a *vehicle*.

These examples show a vehicle entering a building in **garage** and being manoeuvred into position in **park**.

Reverse illustrates the backward movement of a vehicle, and in **follow** and **overtake** it is possible to demonstrate two vehicles in relation to each other.

As with the other representative hand shapes in this section, the hand can 'become' the vehicle, so that it can depict movement, direction and speed. It can move in such a way as to describe driving along a bumpy road, going up a hill, turning left or right, moving off or stopping, and so on.

GARAGE

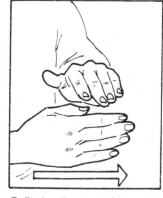

R. flat hand moves to stop under L. bent hand.

PARK (car)

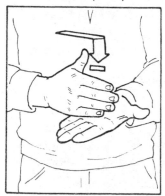

Flat hand moves forward then down onto L. palm, to represent parking a vehicle.

TRAFFIC

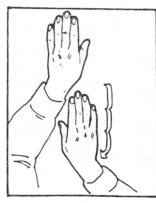

Flat hands held forward, R. behind L. R. hand moves back to body in small hops to indicate line of cars.

REVERSE

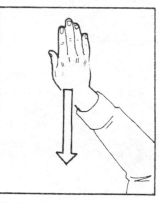

Flat hand moves backwards to represent a vehicle reversing.

FOLLOW (car)

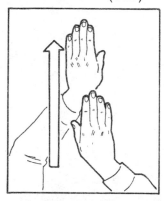

Two flat hands move forward, one in front of the other, representing vehicles.

OVERTAKE

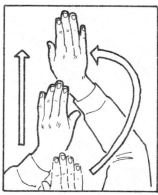

Flat hands move forward, R. behind L., then R. hand sweeps round to 'overtake' the L.

NUMBER INCORPORATION

Some signs can change to give extra information concerning 'number', by changing the hand shape to incorporate the relevant number being referred to.

For example, **we** can be indicated by the extended index sweeping round in a horizontal circle when referring to an indefinite number of people. It is possible to give more specific information by making the same movement with the relevant number of fingers extended, when referring to **we** meaning two, three or four people, as shown in the illustrations.

Which can be similarly modified so that the left (or non-dominant) hand can change to illustrate the number of options being referred to.

Other examples of number incorporation relating to days, weeks and years can be found in Section Six.

WE

Index finger sweeps round to indicate the persons concerned.

WE (2)

Index and thumb extended; hand sweeps round to indicate the persons concerned.

WE (3)

Three fingers extended; hand sweeps round to indicate the persons concerned.

WE (4)

Four fingers extended; hand sweeps round to indicate the persons concerned.

WHICH (of 3)

R. hand little finger and thumb extended; hand moves from side to side behind extended thumb, index and middle fingers of L. hand.

3 YEARS AGO

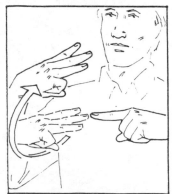

Three fingers of R. hand extended. Hand moves in backward circular movement from tip of L. index.

Section Six

TIME

INTRODUCTION

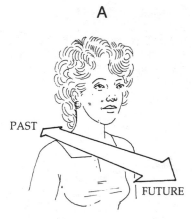

A

To express time in terms of past, present and future and to indicate points in time relative to each other, BSL makes use of space and direction along what researchers call **time lines**.

Firstly, there is *time line A* which involves an imaginary line across the right shoulder. A backward movement over the shoulder expresses past events, and a forward movement expresses future. Forward and backward movements along this line can express passages of time, or points in time relative to others.

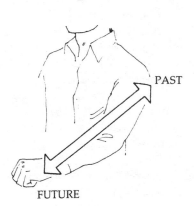

B

Secondly, *time line B*, along the left arm. The arm is normally held loosely at an angle, but for convenience the movements are described as backward for past and forward for future, even though the directions may sometimes appear to be more left and right.

Thirdly, there is *time line C*, which involves an imaginary line from left to right in front of the body and is used to express a continuation of time, particularly sequences of time in relation to each other.

This sounds complicated, but hopefully this section, which looks at these three major time lines, will help to explain it more clearly. Understanding the principles involved is very important in this area of sign language, and may avoid any later confusion.

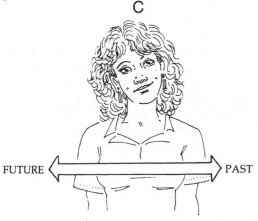

C

TIME LINE A:
THE PAST — BACKWARD IN TIME

Visual imagery in expressing certain time concepts exists in spoken language: we use expressions such as 'cast your mind back', 'back through the ages' and 'looking back to the past', and so on. In relation to future events, we speak of 'what lies ahead', 'forward planning', 'looking forward to the future', and so on. All such expressions present a visual image, as if the speaker were in a fixed point in time, i.e. the present, with past events behind him and future events in front.

This is precisely the principle involved in *time line A* which involves an imaginary line across the shoulder. As pointed out in the introduction to this section, a backward movement over the shoulder expresses past events (a forward movement expresses future).

The illustration for **before (past)** shows this backward movement, and is used to indicate previous events, to refer to things that have happened in the past.

This would be used in contexts such as 'I worked there *before*', '*previous* experience', 'you told me *before*', and so on.

Recently and **long time ago** involve the same backward movement, but are modified to indicate a short time past in **recently**, and a long time past in **long time ago**. Both signs can be further modified to convey 'very recently' or 'ages and ages ago', etc., and facial expression is very important in showing the difference in intensity, as with many other signs.

The illustrations all show flat hands being used to indicate the past, and this is most commonly the case, but the past can also be indicated by the index pointing and moving backward over the shoulder, or by the thumb.

BEFORE (past)

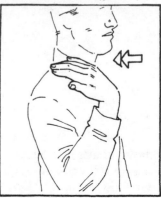

R. hand palm back makes backward movement over right shoulder.

RECENTLY

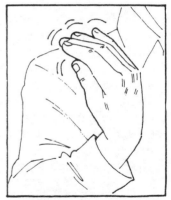

Slightly bend hand makes small backward movement over shoulder. Shoulder moves forward slightly.

LONG TIME AGO

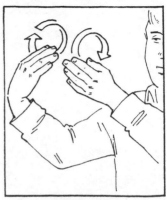

Flat hands circle round each other, backwards over right shoulder.

TIME LINE A: THE PAST — BACKWARD IN TIME

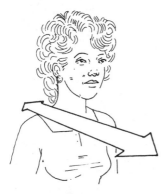

The *backward* movement to express the past occurs again in the signs illustrated here.

Days are indicated at the side of the chin, as pointed out (p.78) in Section Four. The small backward movement in **yesterday** indicates one day past. The same movement, using two fingers in **two days ago** and three fingers in **three days ago**, indicate two days past and three days past respectively.

In some areas, **last week** (not illustrated) is indicated by a backward movement from the side of the chin with the hand in the configuration for 'seven'.

Last year involves a backward circular movement to indicate one year past. The same movement with two fingers extended indicates two years past, and with three fingers extended, indicates three years past, and so on.

These signs also give further examples of how some signs can change to give extra information concerning number by changing the hand shape to incorporate the relevant number being referred to.

YESTERDAY

R. index held on side of chin, drops down/back.

2 DAYS AGO

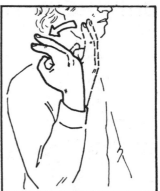

Extended index and middle fingers drop down/back from side of chin.

3 DAYS AGO

Extended index, middle and ring fingers drop down/back from side of chin.

LAST YEAR

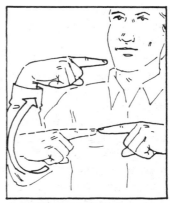

Index tips touch, then R. moves in backward circle, finishing over right shoulder.

2 YEARS AGO

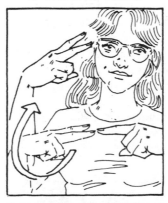

R. hand, index and middle fingers extended, moves in backward circular movement from tip of L. index.

3 YEARS AGO

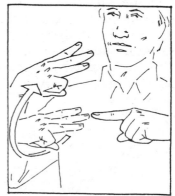

Three fingers of R. hand extended. Hand moves in backward circular movement from tip of L. index.

TIME LINE A: BEFORE IN TIME

BEFORE 1

Two flat hands, R. in front of L.
R. jumps over to finish behind L.

BEFORE 2

R. thumb extended, twists over to
finish behind L. flat hand.

BEFORE 3

Palm back flat hand twists over to
palm forward in forward pushing
movement.

The backward movements looked at so far in time line A relate to time past. The variations of the sign **before** illustrated here, however, indicate a time prior to another and are used to refer to a time that happened, or will happen, before something else.

Before **1** and **2** involve a backward movement along the time line, indicating a point in time previous to another. So, for example, 'Can I see you *before* you go?' is not referring to a past event, but something that has not yet happened. The backward movement implies moving back to an earlier point in time from the event being referred to, which in this example is before someone leaves.

In different contexts, such as '*before* I was married', the same sign would be used, even though the event is in the past, because the importance, in this instance, is the period of time relative to the event referred to, i.e. the marriage. The sign **before (past)** on p. 100 may be added to clarify that it is also an event that happened in the past.

Before **3** has the same meaning, but the movement seems to indicate 'pushing' or 'holding back' the oncoming time as if to stress that an earlier time is being referred to.

These three versions of **before** are all used to indicate a time before another point in time being referred to. They are shown here using time line A, and can be seen later on using different time lines.

This is explained in more detail on pp. 108 and 109.

TIME LINE A: THE FUTURE — FORWARD IN TIME

The previous pages have shown how a backward movement along time line A implies the *past*, or a moment when something occurred or will occur *before* something else. The next few pages show how a forward movement along time line A implies the *future* or a time when something occurred, or will occur, *after* something else.

Future moves forward from in front of the body, to indicate the time ahead. **Since**, however, moves forward from the shoulder, where the past is indicated, implying the passage of time that has elapsed since a previous event.

The forward movement of the right hand in this version of **after** signifies a future time in relation to the present, or to another point in time referred to. For example, 'We'll do it *after*' expresses a forward passage of time from the present. '*After* dinner' and '*after* I left school' express one event in chronological relation to another.

Put off (postpone) implies moving something forward in time.

The forward sweep of the hand in **eventually** and of the index in **later**, signify a forward passage of time. **Eventually** ends on the left little finger, indicating that the passage of time has come to an end.

FUTURE

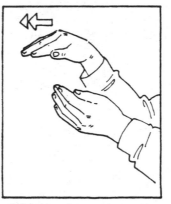

R. bent hand moves forward in two movements; forearm contacts L. hand.

SINCE

Cupped hand moves forward from shoulder.

AFTER

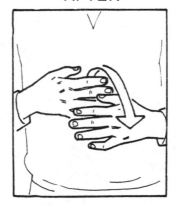

Two flat hands, palms back, R. behind L; R. jumps over to finish in front of L.

PUT OFF

Palm down 'O' hands move in forward arc.

EVENTUALLY

L. little finger extended, R. hand palm down sweeps over and forward to land palm up on L. little finger.

LATER

R. thumb and index extended, thumb in L. palm. Index twists forward then moves forward/down away from L.

TIME LINE A: THE FUTURE — FORWARD IN TIME

The *forward* movement to express the *future* occurs again in the signs illustrated here.

From the side of the chin, where days are indicated, the forward movement of the index in **tomorrow** indicates one day in the future. The same movement using two fingers indicates two days in the future, and with three fingers extended indicates three days in the future, and so on. In some areas 'next week' is indicated by a forward movement from the side of the chin with the hand in the configuration for 'seven'.

Next year involves a forward circular movement to signify one year in the future.

A forward circular movement with two fingers extended indicates two years in the future, and with three fingers extended, three years in the future, and so on.

These are again examples of 'number incorporation', where the hand shape changes to incorporate the relevant number being referred to.

TOMORROW

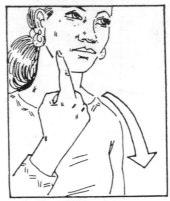

R. index touches side of chin, then swings forward/down, finishing palm up.

IN 2 DAYS

Extended index and middle fingers move forward from side of chin.

IN 3 DAYS

Extended index, middle and ring fingers move forward from side of chin.

NEXT YEAR

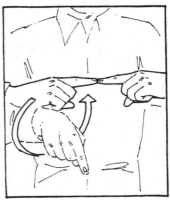

Index tips touch, then R. moves in full forward circle.

IN 2 YEARS

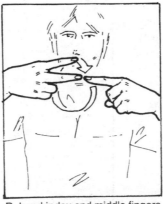

R. hand index and middle fingers extended. Hand moves in forward circular movement from tip of L. index.

IN 3 YEARS

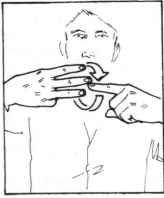

Three fingers of R. hand extended. Hand moves in forward circular movement from tip of L. index.

TIME LINE B: THE LEFT ARM

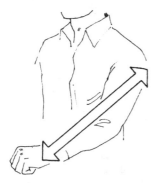

The *left arm* is another significant location in expressing past and future and passages of time.

In some areas, weeks are indicated on the left arm, as illustrated here.

The past is expressed by a backward movement up the arm, as in 'last week', 'two weeks ago', and so on.

The future is indicated by a forward movement down the arm, as in 'next week', 'in two weeks', and so on.

While can be signed with the index or flat hand moving in a forward arc near the wrist to express an ongoing passage of time, or space of time.

This version of **before** is a variation using time line B, based on the top example on p. 102, which used time line A. The indication of a time before a point in time being referred to, as in '*before* I was married', remains the same, even though the sign has been transferred onto a different time line.

LAST WEEK

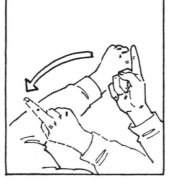

R. index extended, hand moves in arc up left forearm. '2 weeks ago, 3 weeks ago', etc., same movement with appropriate fingers extended.

WEEK

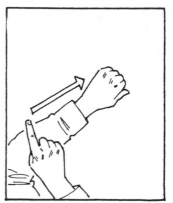

R. index extended, hand moves down left forearm. 'In 2 weeks, 3 weeks', etc., same movement with appropriate fingers extended.

WHILE

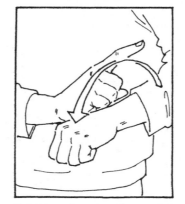

R. index makes a small arc on left forearm, near wrist, like a clock hand moving round.

WHILE

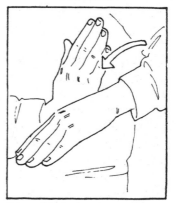

Edge of R. flat hand moves down left forearm in small arc.

BEFORE

Edge of R. flat hand moves up left forearm in small arc.

LONG (time)

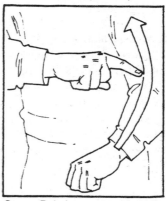

Sweep R. index up extended left arm from wrist to shoulder.

TIME LINE C:
THE CONTINUUM
FROM PAST TO FUTURE

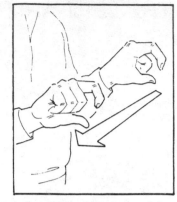

Two 'C' hands move from left to right.

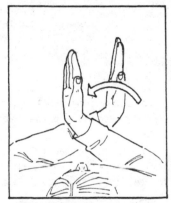

Flat hands held apart, palms facing, R. hand moves to the left in small arc over the L.

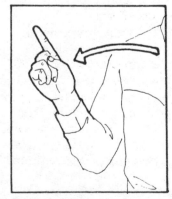

Extended index moves from left to right in front of body in small arc.

This time line involves an imaginary line from left to right in front of the body, which is used to express a continuation of time, particularly sequences of time in relation to each other. Earlier times are indicated to the left (of the signer) and later times to the right.

Continuation of time is indicated in **continue**, moving from left to right, from the past to the future, or from the present into the future.

This left to right movement can also be used to express the passage of time from one point in time to another, or to relate time in sequence.

For example, in a context such as 'I waited from five till six,' a slight movement in the location of the signs (five slightly to the signer's left and six to the signer's right) can convey the passage of time visually.

A movement of the hand, as in 'while,' (p. 105) can be added in between five and six to indicate, or emphasise, the passage of time elapsed between.

In another example, such as 'from 1971 to 1975', 1971 would be made slightly to the signer's left, and 1975 to the signer's right. If reference was then made to *before* 1971, this variation of **before** would be appropriate, as it moves along the same line, and gives a visual indication of a time prior to the one already referred to.

On the same principle, if reference was made to *after* 1975, this variation of **after** would be appropriate, as it moves along the same line and indicates a time later than the one already referred to.

TIME LINE C:
THE CONTINUUM
FROM PAST TO FUTURE

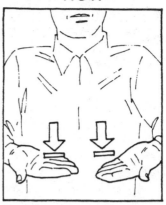

NOW

Flat hands, palms up, move down
with stress.

The present is indicated at a central point along this continuum, as in **now** and 'today'. This can also be seen as a central point on time line A, with the past behind and the future in front.

'Before' and 'after', illustrated on p. 106, can also be used relative to this central point, indicating before or after the present time.

Reference has already been made to the transference of signs onto different timelines. An example of this is the sign illustrated here as **delay**, which uses precisely the same hand shape and movement as 'put off' (p. 103). However, the *direction* of the movement is forward along time line A in 'put off' and from left to right on time line C in **delay**. They are the same sign, but using different time lines. Both imply putting off in time, into the future.

The idea of time continuing indefinitely is conveyed by the forward circling spiralling movement of the index finger moving to the right in **forever**. This seems to be a combination of the forward circular movement used to indicate years and the ongoing continuous aspect of movement to the right, moving into the future.

DELAY

Two 'O' hands, palms down,
move simultaneously to left in
small arc.

FOREVER

R. index points to forehead,
twists and moves forward, then
indexes touch, and R. spirals
away from L.

TRANSFERENCE OF SIGNS ONTO DIFFERENT TIME LINES

On this page, signs are grouped to show more clearly how they can be transferred onto different time lines. The sign and its meaning remain the same, but the starting point and direction change, in accordance with the time line being used.

The first pair show **before 1** making a backward movement on time line A, and **before 2** moving up the left arm, time line B.

The second pair are a different variation of the same meaning and show the forward pushing movement of **before 1**, on time line A, and the same movement being made to the right in **before 2** consistent with time line C. This pushing movement seems to indicate holding back the oncoming time from the future, as if to stress that an earlier time is being referred to.

The third pair show the index moving forward on time line A in **later** and moving to the right on time line C in **after**. Both have the same meaning, i.e. later in time, indicated by a movement into the future on different time lines.

(TIME LINE A) BEFORE 1

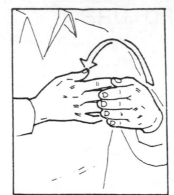

Two flat hands R. in front of L. R. jumps over to finish behind L.

(TIME LINE B) BEFORE 2

Edge of R. flat hand moves up left forearm in small arc.

(TIME LINE A) BEFORE 1

Palm back flat hand twists over to palm forward in forward pushing movement.

(TIME LINE C) BEFORE 2

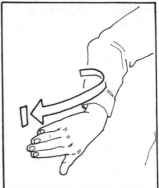

Palm left flat hand twists over to palm right with a pushing movement.

(TIME LINE A) LATER

R. thumb and index extended, thumb in L. palm. Index twists forward then moves forward/down away from L.

(TIME LINE C) AFTER

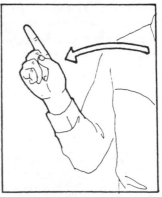

Extended index moves from left to right in front of body in small arc.

TRANSFERENCE OF SIGNS ONTO DIFFERENT TIME LINES

Put off and **delay** provide a pair similar to 'later' and 'after' on the previous page, in that both pairs imply putting off to a future time, as shown by the appropriate directional movement forward in **put off** and to the right in **delay**, along time lines A and C respectively, to a later time in the future.

An indefinite passage of time is indicated in the movement of the flat hand along the left arm, time line B, in **while 1**, and in the left to right movement on time line C in **while 2**.

Until 1 and **2** provide a similar pair, showing the same movement of the right hand ending on the left little finger, indicating that the passage of time has come to an end. The illustrations here show time lines B and C again being used.

Some signs can appear on all three time lines, but for convenience and clarity, these examples have been shown in pairs, to illustrate the basic idea as simply as possible.

(TIME LINE A) PUT OFF

Palm down 'O' hands move in forward arc.

(TIME LINE C) DELAY

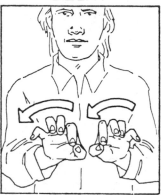

Two 'O' hands, palms down, move simultaneously to left in small arc.

(TIME LINE B) WHILE 1

Flat hand makes a small arc on left forearm, near wrist.

(TIME LINE C) WHILE 2

Edge forward, flat hand moves in small arc from left to right in front of the body.

(TIME LINE B) UNTIL 1

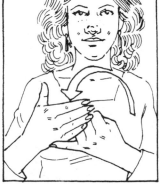

R. flat hand sweeps down left forearm to contact extended L. little finger.

(TIME LINE C) UNTIL 2

R. flat hand sweeps from left to right in small arc to contact extended L. little finger.

FINGER SPELLING

INTRODUCTION

Finger spelling provides a direct representation of the letters of the English alphabet.

The individual letters in the alphabet reproduced on the following page can be compared with the written form of individual letters taught at primary school level. Just as written letters change considerably when written fluently by hand, so finger-spelt letters alter considerably in fluent use. A similar ability to recognise words as 'patterns' also occurs in the fluent use of finger spelling, as it does in the reading of written words.

The use of finger spelling within BSL varies considerably from individual to individual, depending on age, educational background, geographical area, knowledge of English, or personal preference.

Finger spelling can be used to spell out words in full, or to provide an abbreviated form of words, sometimes simply the initial letter.

For some words, such abbreviated forms are so commonly used that they have become signs. In other instances, a finger-spelt formation has been incorporated into a sign.

This section looks at some examples of these different usages.

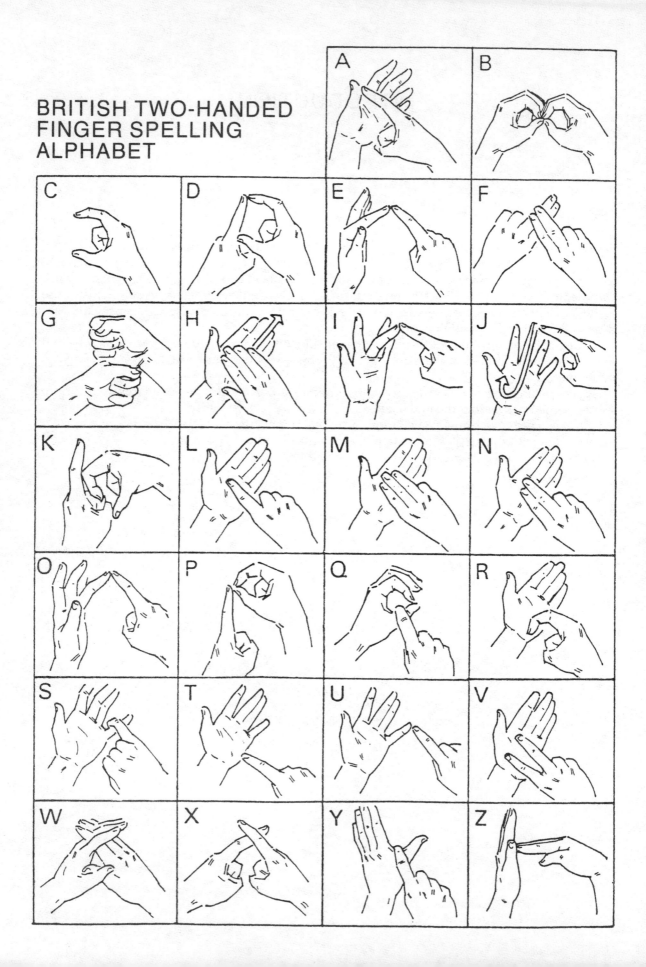

BRITISH TWO-HANDED
FINGER SPELLING
ALPHABET

FINGER-SPELT FORMATIONS IN SIGNS

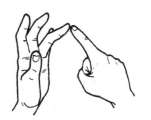

This page shows some examples of signs based on a finger-spelt formation.

Mother, **yellow** and **toilet** involve repetition of the initial letter formation. This repetition seems to echo the spoken words, as does the sign **accident** which involves the first three letters, in a way that mirrors the syllables in the word.

The sign **family** is sometimes made with a palm down flat hand moving in a small horizontal circle. The initialised sign illustrated here is becoming more commonly used; it involves the same movement, with the fingers in the finger-spelt 'F' formation.

English (also used for 'England') involves the right index rubbing along the left — the location of the finger-spelt letter 'E'.

MOTHER

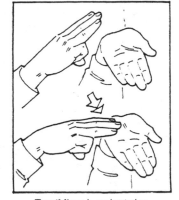

Tap 'M' on L. palm twice.

YELLOW

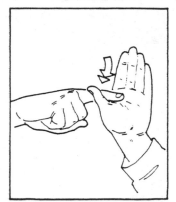

Form finger-spelt 'Y' and brush R. index down slightly, twice.

TOILET

Finger-spell 'T' and tap twice.

ACCIDENT

Finger-spell 'A', then form letter 'C' and move R. hand away to the right in two hops.

FAMILY

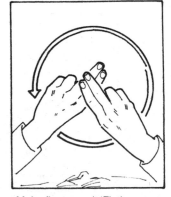

Make finger-spelt 'F', then move formation in horizontal circle.

ENGLISH

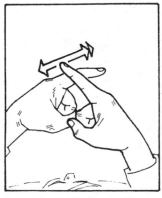

R. index extended rubs along L. extended index several times.

FINGER-SPELT FORMATIONS IN SIGNS

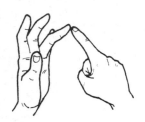

Paper starts with the initial letter 'P', then the fingers make a flicking movement, as if separating sheets of paper.

Qualifications involves the formation of letter 'Q' with a downward movement of both hands.

Leather involves the initial letter making a rubbing movement on the left palm.

About begins with the letter 'A', then the index sweeps round in an arc, across the left finger tips, to form the letter 'T'.

The action of the fingers springing open in **gold** gives an indication of something bright and shiny, following the initial 'G' formation.

The letter 'N' is used in **name**, but instead of its normal position, it is located on the side of the forehead, before twisting and moving forward.

PAPER

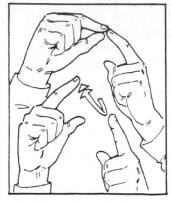

Form finger-spelt 'P', then flick R. index and thumb open twice off end of L. index.

QUALIFICATIONS

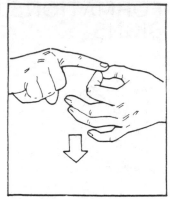

Form finger-spelt 'Q' and make a small movement down.

LEATHER

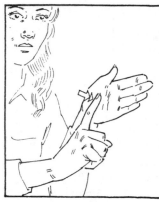

Form 'L' and rub index on L. palm.

ABOUT (concerning)

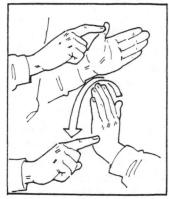

Finger-spell 'A', then sweep R. index finger over L. fingertips to spell 'T'.

GOLD

Form 'G', then both hands spring open and slightly apart.

NAME

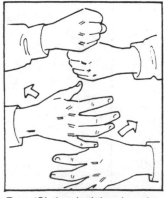

'N' hand touches side of forehead, then moves and twists forward.

FINGER-SPELT FORMATIONS IN SIGNS

The letter 'C' is the only one-handed letter in British finger spelling, and is more easily adapted to form signs than letters requiring two hands in their formation.

These illustrations give examples containing all the normal characteristics of signs, with the additional clarification offered by the hand shape in the initialised 'C' formation.

The alternating hands to and from the mouth in **communicate** convey similar information as signs with related meanings (e.g. 'interview'), with the 'C' hands defining the meaning more specifically.

The 'C' hands in **class** similarly define this sign's meaning more specifically, showing a differentiation between **class** and 'group' (not illustrated), upon which this sign is based, which uses the same movement with a different hand shape.

In **coach**, full 'C' hands are used in a way that gives an indication of the outline, or shape of a coach.

CONTINUE

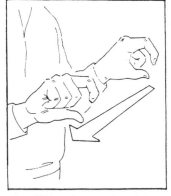

Two 'C' hands move from left to right.

CAREFUL

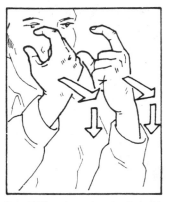

Two 'C' hands, palms back, held under eyes, move forward then down.

COMMUNICATE

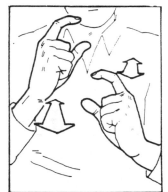

Two 'C' hands, palms facing, move alternately backwards and forwards.

CLASS

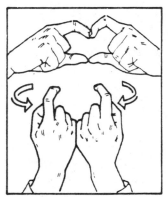

Two 'C' hands touch at fingertips, then swivel from wrists to finish with blades touching.

COACH

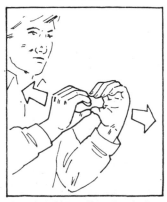

Two full 'C' hands, palms facing, pull apart, L. forward/left, R. backwards/right.

COFFEE

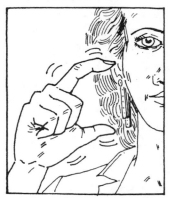

R. 'C' hand palm left waggles from wrist at side of mouth.

117

APPENDICES

APPENDIX

DEAF-BLIND ALPHABET

The R. hand is represented as that of
the sender forming the letters
onto the passive L. hand
of the deaf-blind recipient.

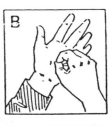

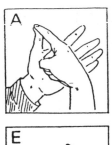

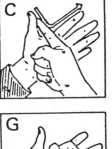

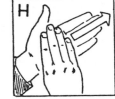

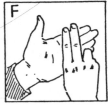

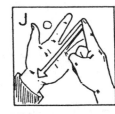

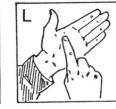

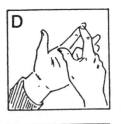

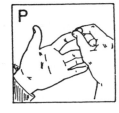

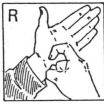

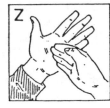

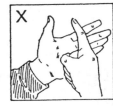

USEFUL ADDRESSES

Alliance of Deaf Service Users and Providers
c/o 5 Arch Road, Great Wymondley, Hitchin, Hertfordshire SG4 7EP.

Association for the Catholic Deaf of Great Britain and Ireland
Henesy House, 104 Denmark Road, Manchester M15 6JS. (Tel: 0161–226 7139 Voice)

Association of British Sign Language Tutors (ABSLT)
39 Rowell Way, Chipping Norton, Oxfordshire OX7 5BD. (Tel: 01608 644468 Voice/ Minicom)

Association of Sign Language Interpreters (ASLI)
92 Picotts End Road, Picotts End, Hemel Hempstead, Hertfordshire HP1 3AT.

Association of Teachers of Lip-reading to Adults (ATLA)
PO Box 506, Hanley, Stoke-on-Trent, Staffordshire ST2 9RE.

Breakthrough Trust
The Hall, Peyton Place, Greenwich, London SE10 8RS. (Tel: 020 8853 5661 Voice; 020 8853 2683 Minicom; Fax: 020 8305 2563)

British Association of Teachers of the Deaf
41 The Orchard, Leven, Beverley, North Humberside HU17 5QA. (Tel: 01863 792890 Voice; 01964 544243 Text; Fax: 01865 792890; e-mail: batod@btinternet.com.)

British Deaf Association
1–3 Worship Street, London EC2A 2AB. (Tel: 020 7588 3520 Voice; 020 7588 3529 Text; Fax: 020 7588 3527; http://www.bda.org.uk   e-mail: info@bda.org.uk)

British Society of Hearing Therapists
Musgrove Park Hospital, Musgrove Park, Taunton, Somerset TA1 5DA. (Tel: 01823 342188 Voice)

Centre for Deaf Studies
University of Bristol, 8 Woodland Road, Bristol BS8 1TN. (Tel: 0117 954 6900 Voice; 0117 954 6920 Text; Fax: 0117 954 6921)

Church of England Advisory Board of Ministry: Ministry Among Deaf People
Church House, Great Smith Street, London SW1P 3NZ. (Tel: 020 7222 9011 ext 329/223 1153 Voice/Qwerty)

Council for the Advancement of Communication with Deaf People
Durham University Science Park, Block 4, Stockton Road, Durham DH1 3UZ. (Tel: 0191 383 1155 Voice and Text; 0191 383 7915 (Text answering machine); Fax: 0191 383 7914; http://www.cacdp.demon.co.uk   e-mail: durham@cacdp.demon.co.uk)

Deaf-Blind UK
100 Bridge Street, Peterborough, Cambridgeshire PE1 1DY. (Tel: 01733 358100 Minicom; 01733 358858 Qwerty; Fax: 01733 358350)

Deaf Broadcasting Council
c/o Ruth Myers, 70 Blacketts Wood Drive, Chorleywood, Rickmansworth, Hertfordshire WD3 5QQ. (Tel: 01923 283127 Voice)

Deaf Studies Research Unit
University of Durham, Department of Sociology and Social Policy, Elvet Riverside 2, New Elvet, Durham DH1 3JT. (Tel: 0191 374 2304 Voice; 0191 374 2314 Text; Fax: 0191 374 4743; e-mail: b.j.clarke@durham.ac.uk.)

'Deafview'
Tim Russell, 19–23 Featherstone Street, London EC1Y 8SL. (Tel: 020 7296 8145; Fax: 020 7296 8021)

The Forest Bookshop: Books, videos, etc. on sign language/deaf issues
8 St John Street, Coleford, Gloucestershire GL16 8AR. (Tel. 01594 833858 Voice and Text; Videophone: 01594 810537; Fax: 01594 833446; Web shopping site: www.Forest.Books.-com   e-mail: deafbooks@forestbooks.com)

Friends for the Young Deaf
FYD Communication Centre, East Court Mansion Council Offices, College Lane, East Grinstead, West Sussex RH19 3LT. (Tel: 01342 323444/312639 Voice/Minicom)

Hearing Concern: The British Association of the Hard of Hearing
7–11 Armstrong Road, London W3 7JL. (Tel: 020 8743 1110 Voice/Minicom; Helpline: 01245 344600 Voice/Minicom; Fax: 01245 280747)

Hearing Dogs for Deaf People
Training Centre, London Road (A40), Lewknor, Oxfordshire OX9 5RY. (Tel: 01844 353898 Voice/Minicom)

Irish Deaf Society
Carmichael House, North Brunswick Street, Dublin 7. (Tel. 00353 1 860 1878)

LASER: The Language of Sign as an Educational Resource
c/o 8 Church Lane, Kimpton, Hitchen, Hertfordshire SG4 8RP. (Tel 01438 832676 Voice and Text; Fax: 01438 833699; e-mail: laser@adept@nildram.co.uk.)

National Association of Deafened People
PO Box 50, Amersham, Buckinghamshire HP6 6XB. (Tel: 01494 723613 Voice/Minicom; Fax: 01494 431932)

The National Deaf Children's Society
National Office, 15 Dufferin Street, London EC1Y 8PD. (Tel: 020 7250 0123 Voice and Text; Parents' Helpline 2pm–5pm: 0800 252380; Fax: 020 7251 5020; e-mail: ndcs@ndcs.org.uk)

'Read Hear'
Jennifer Dodds, CSV Media, 237 Pentonville Road, London N1 9NJ. (Tel: 020 7833 1894 Text; Fax: 020 7833 5689)

The Royal National Institute for Deaf People
19–23 Featherstone Street, London EC1Y 8SL. (Tel: 020 7296 8000 Voice; 020 7296 8001 Text; Fax: 020 7296 8199; Helpline: 0870 6050 123 Voice; 0870 6033 007 Text; http://www.rnid.org.uk   e-mail: helpline@rnid.org.uk)

Scottish Association of Sign Language Interpreters (SASLI)
32 York Place, Edinburgh EH1 3HP. (Tel: 0131–557 6370 Voice and Text; Fax: 0131–557 4110)

Sense: The National Deaf-blind and Rubella Association
11–13 Clifton Terrace, Finsbury Park, London N4 3SR. (Tel: 020 7272 7774 Voice; 020 7272 9648 Text; Fax: 020 7272 6012; e-mail: sense@sense.org.uk)

Sound Advantage plc
1 Metro Centre, Werbeck Way, Peterborough PE2 7UH. (Tel: 01733 361199 Voice; 01733 238020 Text)

TYPETALK: National Telephone Relay Service
John Wood House, Glacier Building, Harrington Road, Brunswick Business Park, Liverpool L3 4DF. (Fax: 0151 709 8119; Helpline: 0800 7311 888 Voice; 0800 500 888 Text; Relay: 0800 959 598 Text; 0800 515 152 Voice; Emergency Relay: 0800 112 999 Text; e-mail: helpline@rnid-typetalk.org.uk)

United Kingdom Council on Deafness
PO Box 13, Abbots Langley, Hertfordshire WD5 0RQ. (Tel: 01923 264584 Voice/Minicom)

Wales Council for the Deaf
Maritime Offices, Woodland Terrace, Malsey Coed, Pontypridd, Mid Glamorgan, Wales CF37 1DZ. (Tel: 01443 485687 Voice, 01448 485686)

BIBLIOGRAPHY AND RECOMMENDED READING

BOOKS

BRENNAN, M., COLVILLE, M. and LAWSON, L. (1980). *Words in Hand: A structural analysis of signs of British Sign Language*. Edinburgh: Moray House College of Further Education.

CONRAD, R. (1979). *The Deaf School Child: Language and Cognitive Function*. London: Harper & Row.

DEUCHER, M. (1984). *British Sign Language*. London: Routledge & Kegan Paul.

EDINBURGH AND EAST OF SCOTLAND SOCIETY FOR THE DEAF. (1985). *Seeing the Signs in Scotland*. Edinburgh: Edinburgh and East of Scotland Society for the Deaf.

EVANS, L. (1982). *Total Communication: Structure and strategy*. Washington DC: Gallaudet College Press.

FLETCHER, L. (1987). *Language for Ben: A deaf child's right to sign*. London: Souvenir Press.

GREGORY, S. (1976). *The Deaf Child and his Family*. London: George Allen & Unwin.

KYLE, J. G. and WOLL, B. (1985). *Sign Language: The study of deaf people and their language*. Cambridge: Cambridge University Press

KYLE, J. G. and WOLL, B. (1983). *Language in Sign: An international perspective on sign language*. London: Croom Helm.

LANE, H. (1987). *When the Mind Hears: A history of the deaf*. London: Souvenir Press.

MILES, D. (1988). *British Sign Language: A beginner's guide*. London: BBC Books.

MINDEL, E. D. and VERNON, M. (1987). *They Grow in Silence: Understanding deaf children and adults*. Second edition. Boston, Mass: College-Hill Press for the National Association for the Deaf.

MYKLEBUST, H. R. (1964). *The Psychology of Deafness*. New York: Grune and Stratton.

ROYAL NATIONAL INSTITUTE FOR THE DEAF. (1981 and 1984). *Sign and Say*. Books 1 and 2. London: Royal National Institute for the Deaf.

SMITH, C. (1992), *Sign in Sight: A Step into the Deaf World*. London: Souvenir Press.

SMITH, C. (1996). *Sign Language Companion: A Handbook of British Signs*. London: Souvenir Press.

SMITH, C. (1999). *Sign Language Link: A pocket dictionary of signs*. Revised edition. Stockton on Tees: Co-Sign Communications.

STERNBERG, M. L. A. (1987). *American Sign Language Dictionary*. New York: Harper & Row.

WOLL, B., KYLE, J. G. AND DEUCHER, M. (1981). *Perspectives on British Sign Language and Deafness*. London: Croom Helm.

VIDEOS

British Sign Language: A beginner"s guide. BBC Video, PO Box 433, Portishead, Bristol BS20 9SG.

Sign 1–10: An Introduction to British Sign Language (BSL). Edinburgh BSL Research Project, Moray House College of Further Education, Holyrood Road, Edinburgh EH8 8AQ.

Introducing Sign: A guide to British Sign Language. School of Education Research Unit, University of Bristol, 22 Berkeley Square, Bristol BS8 1HP.

PERIODICALS

The British Deaf News. Published monthly. Journal of the British Deaf Association, 1–3 Worship Street, London EC2A 2AB.

Hearing Concern. Published quarterly. Journal of Hearing Concern: the British Association of the Hard of Hearing, 7–11 Armstrong Road, London W3 7JL.

See Hear! Published monthly. The Royal National Institute for Deaf People in association with BBC Education.

Talk. Published quarterly. Journal of the National Deaf Children's Society, 15 Dufferin Street, London EC1Y 8PD.

Talking Sense. Published quarterly. SENSE: The National Deaf-Blind and Rubella Association, 11–13 Clifton Terrace, Finsbury Park, London N4 3SR.

For further information about literature on deafness — what exists and how to obtain it — contact: The Royal National Institute for Deaf People, Library, 19–23 Featherstone Street, London EC1Y 8SL. (Tel: 0171–296 8000 Voice; 0171–296 8001 Text; Fax: 0171–296 8199).

INDEX OF SIGNS ILLUSTRATED

127